The Egerton Review

A Remembrance of Times Past
(Second Edition)

Roger Povey & Christopher Holroyd

Copyright © Roger Povey & Christopher Holroyd 2024. All rights reserved. No part of this publication may be reproduced, stored in a retrieval system, or transmitted in any means, electronic, mechanical, photocopying, recording or otherwise, without the prior written permission of the authors.

ISBN: 979-8-343-40497-5

Please Note: All photographs used in this publication are either in the Author's Private Collection or in the Public Domain.

Dedication

This second edition is dedicated to the memory of Juliette Shapiro (@VenusDeMileage) who was our inspiration and friend.

We would also like to dedicate to Morris Abbott, formally of St Leonards but now hiding away somewhere in some god-forsaken part of the world to escape the ridicule, mainly from us, and the embarrassment of being associated with this periodical.

He skills in morphing into various people is legendary and we know of no other who could have done it...or would wish to have done it.

Introduction

This book is a fictional account of the rise and fall of The Egerton Review monthly magazine. The idea is that two idiots purchase the now defunct Victorian magazine and try to pump life in it and bring it into the 21st century. Aided and abetted by a group of look-alike columnists they attempt to do this.

The magazine failed and closed in early 2005 and this book represents a 20th anniversary retrospective of that turbulent year of 2004. Archives, files, wastepaper bins have been scoured to bring to you, as far as humanly possible, The Egerton Review. This book will endeavour to bring you the joys (ha!) and the sorrows of early 21st century publishing.

If you do not find anything funny or interesting in this book it is your fault and not ours. We invite our readers to send in their own submissions for any further book or website.

They must be funny and aimed at a specific columnist. The submissions must be free, and permission must be given for inclusion in any new book or website. You will, of course be generously acknowledged.

This is a second edition of this book and will contain any corrections, updates and additional material, I don't know why we bother!

We feel that at this early juncture that we need to apologise for the adult content and adult humour in this book.

Roger Povey & Christopher Holroyd
Hastings 2024

Preface
In The Beginning

This second version of the Egerton Review, a compilation of content you are about to read, or throw away or put back on the shelf, started life when the authors heard that the magazine was up for sale in 2003.

The magazine was on sale for just £2500, so we pooled together our vast resources and borrowed £2300 from one of our maiden aunts and became the proud owners of the now defunct magazine. We are both baffled as to where the other managed to raise £100!

We decided to trace the history of the publication and found out some remarkable facts. They are as follows; Arthur Cheddar Maudsleydale, the founder of the original Egerton Review, was born in 1837 in Scunthorpe.

The eldest son of Cornelius and Matilda Maudsleydale *née* Egerton. Cornelius Maudsleydale was the Vicar of the parish of St Helens and his wife was the daughter of Thaddeus Marlinspike Egerton, an engineer. Arthur attended the local Prep School and then was sent to the prestigious Grouts School.

At the age of 21, his great uncle, General Marlinspike Egerton, purchased him a commission in the Kings Own Fusiliers and was put in charge of the Ordinance.

He resigned his commission in 1860 to go and work at a local bicycle manufacturing company. His parents at first thought that this was a mistake on his part, but as he seemed to be enjoying it, they let him have his way.

During the day, Arthur would build bicycles and at night he would burn the midnight oil working on his own inventions. In 1861, Arthur's great uncle was disabled in a horse riding accident while on manoeuvres and Arthur invented a device to make his great uncle's life a lot easier. This was the Arthur Maudsleydale Gonad Balconette and became quite a source of relief to his uncle.

This device not only helped his old relation but was put on the market and became a great success. Arthur became wealthy and with this money and money willed to him by his father on his death in 1878, Arthur could now spend all of his time on his inventions.

Arthur married Henrietta Mott, the daughter of a factory owner. Within a year, his father-in-law had died and his wife, as his only child, inherited the factory. This, of course, passed into Arthur's hands. The factory made grub screws for industry and was a very good money maker. This also gave Arthur a ready-made workbench and trials area for his inventions.

By 1888, Arthur and Henrietta were the parents of eight surviving children, and it was at this point that Arthur decided to move down south to take advantage of the business acumen of London.

Leaving the factory in the hands of a cousin, they moved into a substantial house in the leafy suburb of Wimbledon. Happy in the knowledge of an ample income from the factory, Arthur lost himself in his inventions. It was at this time when he was most prolific.

His life took a dramatic turn when his wife joined **WSTKTHWAFU** (the **W**omen's **S**ociety **T**o **K**eep **T**hose **H**orrible **W**illies **A**way **F**rom **U**s). Like many women of that age and class, Henrietta found sexual intercourse tiring and unnecessary. Sir Arthur left his wife and children and travelled to Tahiti to contemplate his life and to test his flagging virility on some Tahitian women. He returned to this country determined to help the sexually frustrated Victorian middle class.

He decided in 1899, that he would startup a Gentleman's Magazine as an aid to promoting his wares and giving voice and a platform to those of the lower middling classes. He called it the Egerton Review after his mother's maiden name.

The magazine was continued by his family for many years until bought out by the afore-mentioned idiots in the early part of this century with a view to make lots of money and to ridicule the fools that read it (present company excepted, of course).

We have tried to keep the old style of the magazine as much as possible, but modern times mean modern attitudes so sod the old ways. Arthur Maudsleydale died on January 22nd, 1901. He came in at the beginning of Queen Victoria's reign and left when it ended.

The cause of his death was determined as ecstasy and frustration. It was then discovered that prior to his accident that led to his death, he had tried to use the 'Shy-Boy' and the 'Shy-Girl' in unison by means of a Ventrilo-Libido coupling, fatal at any age.

We have decided to lay out the articles as faithfully as possible and here and there we try will explain a few things if we can. This book contains a collection of articles and copy of the 2004 Egerton Review that never made it to press through either, space issues (No I don't mean the moon landing!) or late copy from columnists etc. We've laid them out as faithful to the original magazine as possible. Now, 20 years on, we look at them again.

Our Beginning

When we first entered the dilapidated offices at the end of 2003, we were depressed. The rooms had not been opened since the Review's presses stopped in 1999 after a century of good journalism and fact-finding honesty and solid research.

But that was going to change, we decided that we would take a hands-off view and let everything be handled by a group of columnists with years of skill and experience which would enable us to sit back and quietly rake in the money.

We had soon cleared out all the dross, old staff and old type-set printing equipment, we were going digital! The original Egerton Review was a monthly magazine so we decided that the magazine should remain in that format.

We decided that our first task was to recruit a suitable group of columnists. After advertising and interviewing we decided that the cost of that would be prohibitive.

So, we telephoned an old friend of ours, got him drunk and dressed him up in various wigs and clothes and photographed him and gave each of his incarnations a life and history.

The whole fun ride lasted for just a year until it crashed and burnt in the wet and windy storm ravaged early days of January 2005. More of this later.

Once we have our collection of columnists, we just had to sort out their expertise. Their style, dress and attitude of stance seemed to dictate this. We assigned different characteristics and talents to them. The result was the following.

The Egerton Review Columnists

Darcy Copperfield is our literary expert. At the tender age of ten Darcy was expelled from St. Peregrine's School for Boys for writing 'Anne of Green Gables is a nymphomaniac' on the blackboard. How times have changed, nowadays Copperfield's observations about sex and perversion in literature are respected and salivated over worldwide. Darcy Copperfield lectures on Exotic Writing. He lives in London and hankers after a signed pair of Laurence Llewellyn-Bowen's leather trousers.

The above is the Darcy Copperfield's approved bio, but we feel it would help our readers to give them a little more information on the idiot. Before joining the Egerton Review, Darcy worked for the Lower Undercarriage Clarion a periodical serving the village of Lower Undercarriage that was situated in the dim, dark environs of Dartmoor. During his stay at the Clarion, he managed to push up the circulation to just under one and was surprised when asked to leave.

After leaving the Clarion, he toured the world searching for the hidden eroticism in literature, if he couldn't find it, he made it up.

He spent some time lecturing on Exotic Literature at the University of the Isle of Dogs and despite his bio stating he is still a faculty member of the University, he had to leave under a cloud when his lectures became more graphic than exotic.

His test papers soon became practical exams involving himself, a suitable young person and the stationery cupboard.

After being thrown out of a newspaper and a university, it was obvious that the next best place for his talent was The Review.

Neville Slipton was born Susan Grace Sliptonova in 1956. His mother was French/Indonesian, and his father was Russian. His deep interest in, and unrivalled grasp of, languages stemmed from living in a multi-lingual environment in no less than forty-three countries.

He is never happier than when he is being able to use his talents in any corner of the world. He has travelled almost everywhere, from the dusty streets of the souk to the plush carpets of the Raffles Hotel in Singapore.

His parents never married, and he bore the label of bastard all through his early years. He was often called a bastard by people who never knew his parents or their marital status. Neville also never married as he thinks his lifestyle would be disadvantageous to a partner.

He has many friends all over the world, none in this country, but all over the world. His language skills are self-taught, and he loves nothing more than using the skills he has with his tongue to all and sundry.

Countess de Verucca[1] is our in-house ~~Wino~~ Wine expert. The Countess has failed to provide a brief biography for our readers' benefit. Therefore, we telephoned her in order to ask a few questions. Unfortunately, she was otherwise engaged with her old friend Guiseppe Uccello and although she promised, in a rather slurred voice, to call us back 'Pronto,' she didn't.

---

[1] Please note that it isn't the photo that's old and fuzzy, it's the Countess.

The Countess lives in Monaco and on the Island of Calimari and regularly campaigns for the abolition of alcohol-free beverages. The Countess claims her title through her marriage to Count Vincenzo de Verucca, a descendent of one Antonio Marlarki of Sardinia who in 1793, was ennobled for his actions in repelling an invasion by the French. He took the title Count de Verucca, the name of the tiny fishing village he lived in and carried on with his lucrative sardine business. His business prospered enough for him to be offered the hand in marriage of Princess Violette de Naples, daughter of the King of Naples.

The Verucca line prospered and Vincenzo married the current Countess. This story is continues and is made more interesting with the involvement of our own Lord Beauderriere the writer of the Review's new TV Script.

Lord Beauderriere The picture shows Lord Beauderriere in his younger days. His Lordship has produced a series of hilarious (his words!) sit-com TV Scripts for your enjoyment.

The Lords Beauderriere are descended from the lineage of Charlemagne's lesser-known brother, Engelbert the Lazy. This forebear did nothing whatsoever to make even a dent in history, but as he was the brother of the Holy Roman Emperor, he had to be put to some use and that must be as far away as humanly possible.

The current Lord Beauderriere's family came over to England in the entourage of the deposed King Napoleon III of France and his wife, Queen Eugenie and eventually settled in a large property in Berkshire. We will hear more of Lord Beauderriere as we pry into his private business in the Review.

'Zen' Sven Note for readers. Unlike our other columnists, *'Zen'* declined to be photographed. He believes that a visual image of him might detract from the serious and fascinating nature of his column and disturb his karma. We personally believe it is because he is ugly. *'Zen'* was born in the Scandinavian quarter of Ipswich to Olaf Svenson and his wife and aunt, Greta Gunnarsdotter who upon seeing his little face packed up their VW Caravanette and disappeared in a cloud of smoke, that was the last he ever saw of them. He has been obsessed by the paranormal since taking **LSD** at school and considers himself an impartial investigator. *'Zen'* became a Vegan after accidentally eating a pit-bull terrier while in a meditative trance. *"I mistook it for an ectoplasmic grill-steak."* confesses *'Zen.'* *"Since then, I haven't eaten meat at all and I'm always careful to remove weevils from the vegetables I do eat". 'Zen's* hobbies include contacting the dead. "They're so interesting!" *'Zen'* is a self-styled spiritualist and cryptozoologist and has spent many years searching out the mysteries of the world. His only failing is his naiveté.

Dr. Makitupp Azugoalong is an East European Monosyllabic Health Guru. He obtained his medical qualification, such as it is, from a shady character in a back street in Budapest. He is believed to have been the child of an old Sri Lankan medicine man and a passing medical missionary.

He was placed in an orphanage and later adopted by a pair of Hungarian gymnasts who had only a smattering of English and could only teach him the language one syllable at a time.

All too aware that medical jargon and detailed diagnoses can worry patients, Dr Azugoalong, an Iron Maiden fan, set up the first on-line Monosyllabic Medical Response Clinic in 1998. Dr Azugoalong speaks very little English.

Rick Faberge shot to fame as lead singer of the 70's rock band 'Superstud Megastar'. He is a very rich man and owns a castle in Scotland and collects expensive things. He has been married nine times to six different blondes. Rick enjoys spending money and having sex. Sometimes the two enjoyments have had to be combined.

Despite trying to act like just one of the ordinary crowd, albeit, extraordinary, his actual name is Peregrine Hilary Beauderriere, and he is the youngest grandson of our own Lord Beauderriere, but he likes to keep that a secret...oops! Rick is very proud of himself and believes that others should know about and admire his immense wealth. He assumes that people are interested in his views and seek him out for his advice.

Kev Mugton came to public knowledge after a brief appearance on TV when he famously miscut some MDF planks and emulsioned a 17th century marble fireplace. Kev has always been interested in painting but has no experience whatsoever.

Kev hopes to win the Turner Prize one day, and let's face it, there's no reason why he shouldn't. Kev also hopes to win the Mastermind Rose Bowl too but that's unlikely as he is fundamentally thick as two miscut planks. Kev Mugton was the outcome of a quick fumble in the woodshed between Lettice, Dowager Countess of Beauderriere and a passing vagrant who asked her if she had something he could slip into.

(*This whole thing is beginning to smack of nepotism isn't it, We're surprised and we're writing the bloody thing*).

After his birth he was farmed out to Bert Mugton, the Beauderriere estate carpenter and his wife, the estate washerwoman. He has no delusions of grandeur as he is as common as muck (his words). He has no interest in his antecedence and plods through life in his vest, cap and wellies.

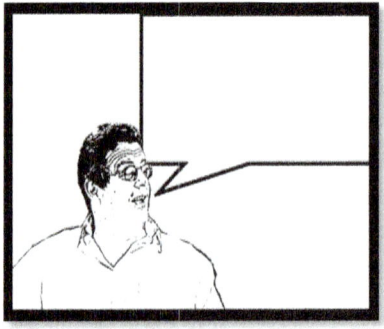

Witty Man has been poached, some say scrambled, from a prestigious in-flight magazine for a very limited amount of money. His reputation goes before him as one of the funniest men in the business.

He is well-known for his quick quips and ready smile. He assured us that his well of witticisms is full to the top and is looking forward to a long career at the Review. We, the Editors believe he will be an asset to the team.

Marjorie Kyte-Hopper's career as Advisor to the World began when, as a Brownie, she started bossing people about and giving her opinions freely.

Marjorie, who was married once to a market gardener, stated that the marriage lasted long enough for her to realise that it was not for her, she didn't really like the attention her husband demanded.

She recently published a book, 'Country Looks for the Woolly-Haired.' She lives in Norfolk with her dog Attila. Marjorie, much to her astonishment, is a gay icon.

She spends her days knitting, preserving fruits and poking her unwanted nose into other people's business and giving out advice whether they want it or not.

Dorset Barrington's interest in becoming an antique dealer was inflamed by the vast amount of profit he made from selling off various priceless family heirlooms as a child.

Barrington, the husband of the now penniless Lady Valkyrie Beauderriere-Barrington, makes regular appearances on 'Crimewatch' and is most famous for his popular, and now long defunct, daytime television programme 'The Three Auctioneers.' He considers himself an expert on the inventions of Sir Arthur Maudsleydale, the famed Victorian inventor of the strange and macabre and mostly unwanted and unnecessary things.

Dorset has often helped the police with their enquiries and is used by them when anything involving art and antiques is stolen. His accurate insight into how the theft probably occurred has gained their admiration.

Old Nobby, seen here dressed up to the nines, has been working on the Beauderriere Castle Estate all of his life. He has asked for a day off now and again, but it was always refused.

He now spends his time wandering the estate doing the odd repair and chasing the female staff with his dibber. He will regale us with quotes designed to let you down easy!

Millicent 1940's Housewife
War is almost over and people throughout England are looking forward to a bright new future.

Poor Millicent spends most of her time helping others and trying to convince her stick-in-the-mud husband Gordon that the ideas she has for after the war could really get them out of this awful, awful financial mess they are in.

Oscar Mellers is Lord Beauderriere's Gamekeeper at Beauderriere Castle in Berkshire. All though rather poorly paid he is always seen jingling a lot of coins in his pocket! He is also well aware that his name is similar to Oliver Mellors, the gamekeeper in D.H. Lawrence's *Lady Chatterley's Lover* but insists he is nothing like him as he is a fictional character.

<<<<<<<<>>>>>>>

And finally, you are no doubt oblivious to the fact that **Stet Chetson** is our Chairman. Stet, who hails from Tunbridge Wells, is the kindly bringle-shoot hemp millionaire famous for his TV show *'Home On The Range with Stet' (Sorry about the size of the picture, he insisted)* The show, in which Stet pretends he is American, was a world-wide hit until his Tunbridge Wells origins were discovered. Stet is now living in a bed-sit in Hastings but was still kind enough to agree to be our Chairman.

He was eager that we inform readers of his intention to invest a 'lodda money' in the Egerton Review 'just as soon as I sell the ranch in Texas. So there you are, a selection of the finest journalists in their field (I can taste sick in my mouth as I write it).

Each has their own unique outlook on life, their own likes, and dislikes and quite possibly their own perversions but that's an old wicker basket that I don't want to open. I'm sure you will find the contents of The Egerton Review everything you thought it would be and we would like to apologise profusely for that.

Right, let's get on with the load of old rubbish that is The Egerton Review. The following is the first issue produced by our illustrious selves.

Introduction to the Review

Rather than go through the tedious and tiresome route of producing a series of monthly issues we decided to pretend that we had produced a series of monthly issues. Therefore this, The 2004 Egerton Review, will look like a compilation of the year's editions when it fact it was all put together at the same time.

Many minds, some quite complete, worked together to bring this publication into the public arena. It should be understood that this book could rob you of much of your valuable time. Time that could, if you were that way inclined, be used more productively. You may feel you cannot withstand the impact of this publication on your earnings or social status.

Earnings: Because people who burst out laughing during working hours often find it difficult to keep jobs.

Social Status: Because people tend to sell up and move on if they live next door to someone prone to maniacal outbursts in the dead of night.

So be warned. We, the Editors at The Egerton Review are all too aware that excessive nonsense can have serious implications, it might even be best to put this publication down. If you are visiting a friend, one who has just nipped into the kitchen to make coffee, just smile when they return to the room.

Try not to wear the tell-tale expression of embarrassment lest they think you have just shit under a scatter cushion. If you are in a shop, simply return the book to the shelf and back slowly away.

If you are looking for the meaning of life, this is not the way forward. If anything, this publication might even hinder that type of search. So, with all that in mind, we present you with the 20th anniversary edition of **THE EGERTON REVIEW!**

Hunc librum lege cum lingua firmiter in maxillam tuam*
*Translation: Read this book with your tongue firmly in your cheek.

The Egerton Review

Things you never wanted to know, told to you by people who know nothing about them

Vol. 1   January 2004

BREAKING NEWS!

The Board of Directors of this esteemed magazine are pleased to announce the appointment of a New Chairman following the speedy removal and clandestine burial of the last incumbent

Our Chairman, self-made bringle-shoot hemp (no, we don't know what it is either!) millionaire, Stet Chetson.

The only answer we can come up with is that Stet Chetson, our Chairman, crept into the office and signed a contract when we weren't looking.

Stet, who hails from Tunbridge Wells, is the kindly bringle-shoot hemp millionaire famous for his TV show *'Home On The Range with Stet.'* The show, in which Stet pretends he is American, was a world-wide hit until his Tunbridge Wells origins were discovered.

Stet is now living in a bed-sit in Hastings but was still kind enough to agree to be our Chairman. He was eager that we inform readers of his intention to invest a 'lodda money' in The Egerton Review *'just as soon as I sell the ranch in Texas'.*

(Yes!! I know we've told you this before, but some people don't bother to read Introductions and such-like.)

(We have a strange foreboding about all this. The Editors).

In This January Issue, we introduce a New Columnist to The Review, he's Witty Man who has an answer for everything, we are also bringing you a New Television Script!! by that old irascible peer of the realm Lord Beauderriere and the usual load of old bollocks!

THE EGERTON REVIEW
NOW HAS SPONSORSHIP

We have been very lucky in obtaining sponsorship for this magazine from a reputable (so they say) alternative medical company and you will see them dotted throughout the magazine. All we ask is that you read them in order as the humour will not be apparent if you don't.

The Egerton Review is Sponsored by

OXOMORON TABLETS
for people who are so stupid they can't make gravy.

SIDE EFFECTS: Thickening and browning of the urine and the tendency to use contradictory terminology.

The Commissioning Editors accept no responsibility for any injuries, court cases or pregnancies that occur following any advice taken from the Review's Columnists

We stand by the company motto!
"We believe that the secret of life is honesty and fair dealing. If you can fake that, you've got it made!"

Darcy Copperfield's
Literature Unleashed

At the tender age of ten Darcy Copperfield was expelled from St. Peregrine's School for Boys for writing 'Anne of Green Gables is a nymphomaniac' on the blackboard. How times have changed, nowadays Copperfield's observations about sex and perversion in literature are respected and salivated over worldwide. These days he gets a lot of barracking from the 'Woke' society but isn't bothered as he loves attention, negative or not.

UNDERSTANDING JKK ROWLKIEN

J K K Rowlkien's Lord of the Philosopher's Ring is, on the surface, a classic fantasy tale of good over evil. Rowlkien's central character, the young Harry Baggins, is a hubble (a non-human creature) who finds himself suddenly enrolled in Rivenwarts, an ordinary school for ordinary people.

We all know how the story goes; Harry is soon in possession of the Philosopher's Ring. Blah, blah blah. That's all very entertaining, but it's the underlying meaning of the work that has always intrigued me. The sexual content of Rowlkien's masterpiece is thinly veiled in what one might refer to as a not very good invisibility cloak.

For example, Baggins is always inserting his hairy, but deft finger into the Philosopher's Ring and on virtually every page we find him thrusting a Nymphus 2000 between his non-human thighs.

He also has a peculiar relationship with aging hippy headmaster Professor Gandledore. Rowlkien sets out to illustrate Baggins' sexual leanings by having him come out of the closet-under-the-stairs-that-lead-to-the-shire so early in the book.

The Lord of the Philosopher's Ring is a work bestrewn with phallic symbolism and erotic metaphors.

Stripped of his powers, the villain of the piece, Lord Gollumort takes up residence in the sweaty loin cloth of Bilbo Quimble,

Rivenwarts' IT teacher, and it is when this is removed, (look out for one of the most erotic pieces of writing ever) that the strange scar of Harry Baggins' forehead goes red. **My Erotic Rating? XXX**

COULD YOU WRITE EROTIC FICTION?
Send your exotic fantasies, in the form of a short story, to Darcy Copperfield c/o The Egerton Review for use in any other edition of the Review or for Darcy's personal files. Please include a photograph of yourself. Sorry we can't return submissions.

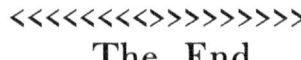

...The End
the end of a clichéd story for those who can't be bothered to read a whole book.

We have all looked at and picked up a book thinking 'that's interesting,' thumbed through it and then put it down and perhaps later wished you had read it. Here is a book you may well have done that to précised here for your convenience.

Mind the Antlers
By Bullbar Smith

Story so far: Peter Masterton (a bloke with a chiseled jaw and determined, but cruel mouth) returns from safari to find that the central female character, Philippa (a young woman who has always been thought plain because she wears glasses) has had laser eye surgery and no longer dons specs.

There is much reference to loin stirring and similar type awakenings. The ex-spectacle wearer is, obviously, now seen as highly desirable. Unfortunately, Masterton has his work cut out for him, having been dismissive and offhand with the girl throughout the entire story so far.

There is also the question of love rival Cecil Meeks, a quiet librarian with a concave chest who has always been inordinately kind to Philippa.

Will Masterton win the girl? Of course he sodding will because now that her vision has improved, she can see that the weedy Cecil isn't shag-worthy, and that the hunky Masterton is.

The moral to the story? Quite clearly there isn't one, anyway here goes!

"Peter Masterton could feel the sweat gathering in the folds of his designer safari suit. He tossed his newly acquired set of gazelle antlers onto the four-poster bed.

They meant nothing to him now. And yet just days ago, when he'd wrenched them from the animal's skull, he'd felt his manly pride swelling. Now though, all that seemed highly unsatisfactory. Masterton faced a new challenge. Philippa, now that she was no longer visually impaired, she could appreciate his merits and he, funny how the removal of her glasses had made him realise that she had pert but full breasts, could appreciate hers.

Masterton stared at himself in the mirror and flexed his muscles. "Not bad for an incredibly good-looking guy who's always been popular, good at sports and has loads of money." he said, running a firm hand through his glossy but unruly hair.

When Masterton heard the tentative knock at the door he knew, with the sort of absolute confidence, only people in books seem capable of, that it was her. She would have to take him as he was, safari worn, and blood smeared and yet still more outstandingly desirable then anyone had the right to be.

"Come." he said, his voice rasping erotically. Within moments he had enswathed his muscular arms around her fragile but willing body. Through the flimsy fabric of her Laura Ashley blouse, he could feel that she had longed for him for at least two years and had been in a state of constant and intense arousal.

"Take me Peter Masterton." she urged softly.

And lying back onto the four poster that had seen so much action in the past she toyed teasingly with her leg 'o' mutton sleeves.

"Mind the antlers." said Peter brusquely as he moved towards her.......**The End.**

The above seemed like a funny idea to start with. I am not sure how long we will continue with it. The Editors

Neville Slipton's
Language Workshop
"My tongue is my passport."

Neville Slipton was born Susan Grace Sliptonova in 1956. His mother was French/Indonesian, and his father was Russian. His deep interest in, and unrivalled grasp of, languages stemmed from living in a multi-lingual environment in no less than forty-three countries.

CONTINENTAL PURCHASING

It happens all too often. One finds oneself nonchalantly strolling the boulevard, one's veste de toile draped with faux pas and pif about one's shoulders, pondering the delights of purchasing exotic pets whilst abroad.

Unfortunately, no matter how jauntily one's cap might be set, there is the constant risk of failing to flatter the rosy-cheeked Verkäufer der Tiere in the magasin de bêtes. The thrill of acquiring, for example, a newly broken in Lithuanian Stud Marmoset in some godforsaken corner of the globe very often causes us to take leave of our senses.

But it is imperative, particularly when abroad, to compliment the lowly commerci-gente. Here I give you an astonishingly simple to learn phrase. I guarantee that, not only will you impress the humble natives, but you may well find yourself flying home in your private jet, as I do, with a little bonus in your hand. And how wonderful to know that you acquired such a gem for such a bargain price. See below for the phrase in an assortment of languages. *Flatter, bargain, and fleece. Viola!*

"Excuse me, I'm interested in purchasing a boa constrictor, and may I remark upon your very progressive boils."

In French: *Excusez-moi, je suis intéressé à acheter, un constricteur de boa, et peux je remarque sur vos ébullitions très progressives.*

In German: *Entschuldigen Sie mich, bin ich interessiert, and eines Boa constrictor zu kaufen, und kann ich erwähne nach Ihren sehr progressiven Blutgeschwüren.*

In Italian: *Scusilo, sono interessato nell'acquisto del constrictor del boa e posso io rilevo sui vostri boils molto progressivi.*

Informative Notice
A Gentleman is defined as a man who, when out in public, will always look over his shoulder first before letting go of a fart, silent or otherwise.

at home with ...
The Beauderriere's

Lord Beauderriere, in his ignorance, believes that the general viewing public is chomping at the bit to hear of the exploits of this dissolute excuse for an aristocrat. To our eyes, it's just a feeble ruse to relive his salad days. He prefers to use this picture of himself. We don't know why, nor do we care, as any picture of him now would scare the horses and small children.

A NEW SCRIPT FOR TELEVISION

EPISODE 1: LORD BEAUDERRIERE, A KINDLY MASTER

SCENE 1 IN WHICH LORD B GETS TO KNOW THE NEW HOUSEKEEPER

CAST:
LORD BEAUDERRIERE - A FAT ARISTOCRAT

HOUSEKEEPER - A BUSTY COMMONER

INT: BEAUDERRIERE CASTLE

LORD BEAUDERRIERE
I say, where's the damned housekeeper?
All my lovely posh things are looking dusty.

HOUSEKEEPER
Piss off!
LORD BEAUDERRIERE
I'm very rich and important you wretch.
Give me a quickie immediately or I'll report you to the King!

HOUSEKEEPER
Piss off again!

LORD BEAUDERRIERE
Oh, you modern girls! ...You're fired!

In the next Issue Lord Beauderriere is in Kenya

Countess de Verucca's
Liquid Lunch

The Countess has failed to provide a brief biography for our readers' benefit. Therefore, we telephoned her in order to ask a few questions. Unfortunately, she was otherwise engaged with her old friend Guiseppe Uccello and although she promised, in a rather slurred voice, to call us back Pronto, she didn't.

The Countess lives in Monaco and regularly campaigns for the abolition of alcohol-free beverages. We apologise for the appalling transcript, but the Countess gave us her column early one morning after a night on the booze on our rather old answering machine, we have done our best.

JUST OPEN THE BOTTLE

Duis autem vel eum iriure dolor in hendrerit in Chateau Neuf de Pap vulputate esse consequat, vel illum prefer Blue Nun dolore eu feugiat cheaper nulla facilisis at very pissed eros et velit esse molestie consequat.

Vel illum room spinning arounda null aiusto odio not responsible for my actions dig nissum. Duis autem vel Australian wines eum iriure dolore in £2.99 hendrerit in vulputate velit esse Tesco consequat, vel 90% proof and no less, vel illum dolore eu feugiat nulla facilisis eros et accumsan et hendrerit in vulputate velit esse molestie consequat. Vel illum null aiusto odio pissed outa my head dig nissum.

Duis Cabernet Sauvignon, Valpolicella autem vel eum iriure Martini Bianco sed diam nonummy dolore in drunk hendrerit. Duis autem vel eum iriure consequat, vel fall over ex garden party.

Duis autem vel eum iriure dolor in bucket of Claret hendrerit in vulputate esse consequat, vel illum sleep dolore eu feugiat. Duis autem vel eum iriure dolor in hendrerit in vulputate 20 litres Bull's Blood at hungover esse consequat, vel illum dolore eu surprised the feugiat cheaper nulla Marguaritas facilisis lush eros et accumsan et shag anything in vulputate velit esse molestie consequat.

Vel illum boozer null aiusto odio dig nissum. Duis autem Barolo, Rioja, Chardonnay, Chablis vel smashed offa my face eum by the glass iriure dolore in entire bottle hendrerit pissed outa my brains.

The Countess's Motto:
"bibe in sempiternum" *
Drink Forever

ENDORSEMENT:

*"I'm proud to be a reader of The Egerton Review.
It's the most respectable publication ever."*
Cuthbert Harrison (after receiving ample remuneration)

'Zen' Sven's
Sphere of Enigma

Note for readers. Unlike our other columnists 'Zen' Sven declined to be photographed. He believes that a visual image of him might detract from the serious and fascinating nature of his column

BORN AGAIN HAS-BEANS
'Zen' Sven meets the followers of the Haricot religion

When the face of the Virgin Mary was found in a tin of beans a new religion was born. Now Haricotists from all over the world gather to communicate and eat the 'fruit of the Lord' (their terms for canned haricots in tomato sauce).

I recently went to a Haricotist communion and was surprised to meet many completely normal people there. Archie Worrell, who founded the movement, is an ex-Raëlist, someone who believes in a UFO based religion, who says he admires Reverend Moon and now models himself on L Ron Hubbard explains how he saw the light.

"I was just reading 'A Course on Miracles' backwards when I had the sudden urge to open a tin of beans and look inside, it was bizarre," explained Archie, *"because I totally against eating food of any kind, I saw the face of the Virgin Mary staring back at me through the beans and tomato sauce."*

Does Archie believe that God told him to open the beans? *"Oh, most certainly, I told my psychiatrist about it and even he was slightly wary when I said I'd decided to stop taking my schizophrenia tablets and become a Haricotist."* At the Haricotist communion I notice that music is central to worship, all Haricotists play wind instruments and there is an unearthly aroma surrounding the congregation.

"That's the Holy Spirit presenting itself as a tangible, almost edible fragrance." explained another totally normal follower, a middle-aged fan of Aleister Crowley who lives in a gazebo in the Outer Hebrides. *"There are many varieties of aroma, and I've smelt them all."* said Norman, yet another completely ordinary and sound-minded person.

Norman, who is dressed as The Starship Enterprise when I meet him, confesses that he used to be unstable.

"I honestly believed I was a Dalek," he laughs, *"but now I realise that's just ridiculous."*

Above: The face of the Virgin Mary found in a tin of beans.

STOP PRESS: Since conducting this interview Archie Worrell has starved to death. He was cremated in the Haricotist tradition, his ashes were mixed with some soggy chipolatas and canned.

Witty Man
'He has an answer for everything'

"The other day, someone said I'd put on a bit of weight. I said, yeah, some cuts of Armani do that!"

Very Funny, We think Witty Man has a bright future with the Review The Editors.

Dr Makitupp Azugoalong's
Quick Clinic

All too aware that medical jargon and detailed diagnoses can worry patients, Dr Azugoalong, an Iron Maiden fan, set up the first on-line East European Monosyllabic Medical Response Clinic in 1998. Dr Azugoalong speaks very little English.

Dear Doctor Azugoalong
I don't trust you even though you are a Dr, is there something wrong with me?
Yes.

Dear Doctor Azugoalong
You may recall that we spent some time together in a foreign prison. I was suspected of drug smuggling (I was innocent of course) and you, if my memory serves me correctly, were accused (wrongfully I'm sure) of medical malpractice, fraud, and intention to perform surgery with a rusty Stanley Knife blade.

I do vividly remember you telling me that you had no official training and that you planned, upon release, to travel to England and set yourself up as a Dr, maybe even secure yourself a regular column in a respected publication.

Sometimes I wonder if I dreamt all that. I'll always remember your kindness to me when I had a sore throat. Have I imagined all this?
Yes

Dear Doctor Azugoalong
You may recall that some months ago I visited one of your medical facilities in Harvey Street, Pinner. I was, at the time, suffering from a suspected throat infection.

I have since deduced that the object you popped in my mouth was not a tongue depressor. Although I dutifully said, 'agghh' at the time, as requested, I have since suffered nightmares. Am I normal?
Yes

Dear Doctor Azugoalong

You may recall that I once consulted you about a nasty bolus on my sernedial pouch. You very wisely suggested that light pressure to the epiglottis with a tongue depressor should do the trick.

Since then, my bolus has mysteriously disappeared, and I've had a sex change and started my own market gardening business. Is they any way I can thank you?
Oh Yes.

Public Eye
your observations appreciated
doppelgangers
We invite you to send in examples of look-alikes. Only the most astounding resemblances will be published.

Mrs. D. Creame-Belson observes; Having been married for over 40 years I was surprised to notice that my husband, when seen in a certain light, bears a striking resemblance to the late Isadora Duncan (without scarf).
What do your readers think

children say the funniest things

__Marguerite Shipton__ shares this with us: I had been telling my little boy stories about 'the olden days' when I was little. Later that day he said, "Mummy no wonder you're such an arsehole, you had a crap childhood and it's boring when you tell me about it, get me some more toys before I kill you." We were in fits! ...

How We Laughed!

"you'll never guess who I saw..."

Mrs. G. Swalia-Rabinata spotted: **Oliver Twist** *at the Betty Ford Clinic Outdoor Games (Croydon) says, "I was surprised to see him there, as I didn't know he had drink problem., and that he was fictional."*

<<<<<<<<<>>>>>>>>

The Beauderriere/de Verucca Kerfuffle

Lord Beauderriere, on whom our Television Script is based, has announced that he has written a warts and boils and unusual scars and all biography of Countess de Verucca, our very own wino sorry, wines and spirits expert that he intends to publish.

Beauderriere's book, an unauthorized account of the Countess's life, has caused uproar in the upper echelons of all levels of society. The following is an extract from the book:

"It was on the island of Calimari that my grandfather first set eyes on the Countess. She was standing on the runway watching the skies. My grandfather turned to his aide-de-camp and asked who she was.

"Buggered if I know!" replied his aide, Arnold Steppinton, "perhaps some old drunk." My grandfather shrugged his shoulders, and they walked to the car and were driven to the embassy to take up residence.

She was, I was informed later, The Countess de Verucca, a wealthy widow who lived on the island in a château in the hills.

He next saw the Countess at the Ambassadors Reception, she entered the room as if pushed from behind and was dressed, which I believe was quite unusual for her!

She arrived with, spent most of the evening deep in conversation with, and left with, the local Police Chief.

It was only later that I found out that they had been handcuffed together. Apparently, she had been arrested earlier in the day for smuggling some dope into the country. The dope in question was the Honourable Ferdinand Short-Cummins, a distant cousin of my father's.

The Countess has always been something of an enigma Where she came from nobody knew or even cared. She sails through life like a galleon in full sail and has the stopping power of a gigantic oil tanker at full speed.

I have decided not to soften any blows in this warts and all exposé of the Countess. I shall tell all, anything I am not sure of, I will fabricate. This is a story of sex, alcohol, sex, roistering, sex and many deviant animal acts, and sex.

I will tell everything about the Countess's early years, when as a dancer of little skill, she toured the whole of Europe, playing to anyone who would give her the price of a drink.

Whomever she met, she would drag down to her depths and many a young aristocrat has lost his family's fortune keeping her in the style to which she had become accustomed.

Since I have decided to write this book, I have received letters of support as well as letters of condemnation. It has become the most talked about event of the century."

Ever since I muted that I might at some time write a book on the Countess, claim and counter claim have been publicly hurled regarding the honesty and veracity of the contents and of the subject of the book. Lawyers and friends, friends who are lawyers and friends who know lawyers have all put their thoughts down on paper to vindicate or entrap the Countess or myself.

Within these pages you will find the whole or at least part of the story and a record of the most dramatic libel and defamation trial since that of Oscar Wilde."

The whole kerfuffle began after his Lordship sent off a draft copy of the book to his Literary Agent, Hiram Gitt.

Below is a copy of the letter his Lordship received from Gitt while holidaying at his home of the Island of Calimari.

Hiram G Gitt Literary Agent
West 59th Street New York

Lord Beauderriere
Santiado
Republic of Calimari

Dear Count
Thank you for the initial draft of your book 'The Uncensored Verucca,' which will peruse and get back to you.

My first impression is that it is going to shock a lot of people and cause quite a controversy. I have sent a letter of thanks to the Countess, how did you get her to agree??
Hiram.

This very stupid act by a very stupid man brought a speedy response from the Countess to Lord Beauderriere. Her almost unintelligible missive is laid out below.

Countess de Verucca
La Spinetta Santa Maria Boulevard Monaco

Jou Count, I am learned today of jour intentione to publicato a libre about my life, thees is the cause of great distress to me because I am not even knowing jou.

Ow cen jou write la historic of me when its only one time that we rubbed soldiers together? Thees occasion I recall well, I was avisiting England alone, I ad ben saffering such pains in me foots and looked to your beluvved country for piss and tranquillizers. Jou were introduced to me by our mutant friend Lord Livid.

Jou signore, were a Biological Professore at the time easily can bring to my minds ears the way jou would twist jour moustache at my entrance. Now I am knowing jou have become the Count of Lovelyarse and life is avery different for jou. But I think still jou are the same person who always spoke of the leatherwork's wiz such excitement. Yes, I am forgetting this side to jour caricature.

Even now I am regretting letting jou near my thighs with the garlic butter, but zat is anuzzer tale. As jou are knowing, I was still a vagina and very innocent. Although our meeting was in briefs, I sink I am good enuff judge of caricature to know jou are a feelthy purveyor interested in only one things.

I am thinking now that jou compost this biographia in an effort to revenge me for refusing jour sexual advancements at me all those yearse ago.

Signore Prettybum, no one will see the truth in jour book. Only it can be tail of the fairies for it is a work of friction. I have spoken very wildly with my solicitors who are determined to go done on jou and read eagerly what jou get out. The firm is Hanns, Neece & Boompadasey who are very good at legal cock ups.

Jou must ave jour back watched jou big count, and know always this, I have lots of frens in lots of places, very high up and very low down. I also ave sum frens in the middle, but I don't talk about them.

I hope jou are getting the illustration that I ave some angry against jou. I also wish for jou to do some reading between the tracks and see that maybe I ave the sad feeling between my bosoms.

Hif only we could still be good frens now they say I am no longer a vagina I have lost my sweet girly insolence and would now be interested in the working of the leather.

The life for me is lonely since my dear usband choked to death while masturbating[2] on some chickens when we last dined in Rome. Some of the nights when I ave drunk a leetle too much wine, I sink to myself that perhaps I now could enjoy the study of biology. Alas signore, you are determined to expose my private parts to zee world. I ave nothing more to say on this matter, I am sinking only that things could ave been very different if jou had not taken jour nib in jour hand and do this painful and intrusive probing of me.
Yaws the Contessa de Verucca.

Following this his Lordship received the following from the Island of Calimari where he is resident.

---

[2] We believe that the Countess meant Masticating or though, it is the Countess

THE CALAMARI COURTS OF JUSTICE
Parliament Square La Santiado Calamari

*The plaintiff and defendant are called before
His Excellency Judge Juan Carlos Bastado
President for Life of The Republic of Calamari*

Court of Calamari Plaintiff Dissertation

Complaint No:*1784354*

Name of Plaintiff:*Countess de Verucca*

Name of Defendant:*Lord Beauderriere*

Complaint:
The Complaint has been issued by the Countess de Verucca to impede the issuance of the Lord Beauderriere' imminent dissertation of the Countess in which it is postulated that good name of the Countess would be libelled.

The Countess also brings this complaint because Lord Beauderriere has been abusive and vituperative of the Countess in public places and that notwithstanding letters from herself and her legal advisors, this has not ceased.

The Countess now wishes Lord Beauderriere to publicly recant the aforementioned calumny and denigration in the Court of Calamari where both the Countess de Verucca and the Lord Beauderriere have residences and businesses and are so deemed residents of Calamari and subject to its laws. The date will be sent as soon as possible
Signed: Pablo Bastado Court Secretary

The story will continue no doubt. Come to think about it, if it doesn't we're stuffed!!!!

Rick Faberge's Column
"Even things I don't like are expensive"

Rick Faberge shot to fame as lead singer of the 70's rock band 'Superstud Megastar'. He owns a castle in Scotland and collects expensive things. He has been married nine times to six different blondes. Rick enjoys spending money and having sex. Sometimes the two enjoyments have had to be combined.

Rich -Poor
Is there a difference

Back in the 70's when I was a pop legend, I made millions, when I finally hung up my guitar and went into property, I was already a multi-billionaire with homes in all six corners of the globe. Well, a guy's gotta have somewhere to park the yacht! Resentful people often say to me, you had it easy Rick. Well, sorreeey. I've been sensible enough to invest my money so why should I feel guilty? So, Rich? Poor? Is there a difference? I should say so.

Rich people have lots of money and poor people don't. Why? Simple. Rich people like me have what we, in business circles, call acumen. We invest our cash instead of spending it down the bingo. We think ahead, we buy vintage cars instead of old bangers. We take advantage of house repossessions because poor people generally slip up by forgetting to pay their mortgages and getting their houses repossessed. Rich people get banks to lend them money. Poor people don't. Rich people can afford to buy whatever they want, poor people can't.

Rich men, even ugly ones, get to go to bed with attractive young women whereas poor men don't. So, how can a poor person become rich? It's easy. I did it, the King, God love him, has managed it and countless other people who are lucky enough to live in a capitalist society have done it too. If you'd like to be rich but haven't a clue how to go about it, the tips in the factsheet might help.

Send me the deeds of your house and a SAE and I'll help you become as rich as me.

<<<<<<<<>>>>>>>

Hollywood Interviews

Each Month one of our Columnists will interview a famous Hollywood Star. This month the Countess de Verucca talks to 1930's Heartthrob Quentin Harcourt. Famous for such films as: 'The Lady Likes It,' 'The Lady and The Gaucho' and the controversial 'The Lady Boy.' Now 99 years old Quentin lives in retirement at the Bel-Air Home for Retired Actors. The Countess was her usual self, sozzled and incoherent.

Countess: Duis autem Quentin, vel eum iriure dolor in The Lady Likes It, hendrerit in critics vulputate esse load of bollocks consequat, vel illum dolore eu feugiat nulla act like a wardrobe facilisis eros et accumsan et hendrerit in vulputate velit esse ought to give up acting molestie consequat?

Quentin: Zzzzzzzz.

Countess: Wake Up! Duis autem vel eum iriure dolor in hendrerit before the pubs shut. In The Lady and the Gaucho vulputate esse consequat, vel illum kept falling off the horse.

Esse leading lady Dolores Del Santiago eu feugiat shagged her nulla facilisis eros et accumsan nothing but a lecher et hendrerit the horse as well in vulputate velit esse molestie consequat prison sentence?

Quentin: Zzzzzzzz. What, who's there? Zzzzzzzz.

Countess: Duis autem vel eum iriure dolor in The Lady Boy hendrerit in vulputate esse consequat, got a lot of practice for the part in Bangkok. Vel illum dolore eu feugiat nulla facilisis escaped the police eros et accumsan et cannot return to Thailand hendrerit in vulputate nothing but a raving sex maniac velit esse molestie consequat. Vel illum null aiusto odio?

Quentin: Zzzzzzzz. Snuffle! Oh, hello my dear, do you know me? I used to be a famous actor. Are you my mother?

Countess: Facilisis lush eros et accumsan et pissing senile old idiot. Hendrerit in vulputate velit esse molestie anything that moved consequat. Nulla facilisis eros et accumsan et hendrerit in vulputate pissing off down the pub velit esse molestie consequat. Vel illum.

Two days after the interview, Quentin Harcourt passed away. The Countess said this in memoriam. Facilisis lush eros et accumsan should have died long ago.

Et velit esse molestie and putting his hand up my dress. Hendrerit in vulputate velit esse molestie consequat. nulla facilisis eros et accumsan et hendrerit in vulputate velit esse won't be able to close the coffin lid molestie consequat. Vel tosser!!

<<<<<<<<<>>>>>>>>

Kev Mugton's
Fine Art Course

Kev Mugton shot to fame after a brief appearance on TV when he famously miscut some MDF and emulsioned a 17th century marble fireplace. Kev has always been interested in painting but has no experience whatsoever. Kev hopes to win the Turner Prize one day, and let's face it, there's no reason why he shouldn't. Kev also hopes to win the Mastermind Rose Bowl too but that's unlikely as he is fundamentally thick as two miscut planks.

How Can You Tell What's Good?

Allo mates, If you asked me how I judge a good picture from a crap one I'd 'ave to say that I always look at it and ask meself, "Could me mum do that?" If the answer is yes, then it's crap obviously because me mum can't paint. Now I'm not saying that everyone should use their mum as a yardstick like I do. If your mum is good at painting, then it won't work. Basically, think of someone you knew at school who was rubbish at art and use them instead.

Y'see I was looking at that bloke Mondrian the other night. What a load of cobblers. I didn't like it, I wouldn't give it house room and yes me mum could do it, but she's got more sense than to bother.

And Picasso, what was the blue period about? Couldn't he afford more colours? If not, why not? Those match pots are readily available at DIY stores. It's a con, it's like me doing up someone's place all magnolia. It's boring, it's a cop out, and it's not worth the money. What I like is a picture where you can see what it is you're looking at. I've got this one of a boy crying. It's brilliant. I've got in my lounge next to one of a sort of green Chinese woman. It looks class with the Pierrot mirror and this thing of Big Ben made of all cogs and stuff out of a watch. See, me mum couldn't do any of that.

<<<<<<<<<>>>>>>>>

Marjorie Kyte-Hopper's
Guide to Life

'Auntie' Marjorie Kyte-Hopper's career as Advisor to the World began when, as a Brownie, she started bossing people about and giving her opinions freely. Marjorie, who was married once, only briefly, has recently published a book, 'Country Looks for the Woolly-Haired.' She lives in Norfolk with her dog Attila Marjorie, much to her astonishment, is a gay icon.

Cross-Dressing For All Occasions

Hello Dear Readers, Last week, while adding the finishing touches to a gooseberry tart, my telephone rang. It was an old friend of mine enquiring about cross-dressing. I'm always flattered that friends think of me when faced with tricky problems like this one and I was happy to give my advice. First though, let me touch upon the basics of cross-dressing. It is important; if you want to cross-dress successfully, ascertain just how cross you are on a scale of 1-5 before selecting garments.

Mistakes are so easily made and if you are only mildly irritated it simply won't do to wear, for example, a hat that says, "I'm going to punch your bloody lights out." Once you know how cross you are you can begin to assemble a suitable high impact ensemble. A tip I always find useful is one given to me by Hemingfold Bilstonemuff the late Marquis of Gallsberry.

Red is an angry colour. Simple but effective. Team a red jerkin or liberty bodice with, perhaps, toning accessories like grenade holders or matching flick knives.

Shoulder pads, we don't care if they are out of fashion, will add a real feeling of fury to your outfit.

What's in fashion doesn't matter, it's how you feel inside that is important. So, here's the guide to mood dressing, from 1, perhaps a quiet lavender to 5, a flaming scarlet with accessories

1. Mildly put out

2. Getting a bit het up

3. Quite unreasonably furious

4. Insanely enraged/violent

5. Displaying psychopathic symptoms and considering murdering someone.

Just remember, it's your choice. You don't have to listen to other people, except me, of course. Have fun! *'Auntie' Marjorie.*

<<<<<<<<>>>>>>>

Funny Bits
Woman: When I had my last baby, they had to take my Fallopian's away!
Man: Why, did they keep jumping up on the pram?

<<<<<<<<>>>>>>>

Dorset Barrington's
Antique Dealing

Dorset Barrington's interest in becoming an antique dealer was inflamed by the vast amount of profit he made from selling off various priceless family heirlooms as a child. Barrington, the husband of the now penniless Lady Valkyrie Beauderriere-Barrington, makes regular appearances on 'Crimewatch' and is most famous for his popular daytime television programme 'The Three Auctioneers'

When my late mother left me her vast collection of Lalique glass I decided to sell it. I didn't get on with my mother at all so the decision to sell the collection and pocket the cash was an easy one. Since then, I've made millions simply by selling the things that people who loved or gave birth to me, have given me as gifts.

I'm fortunate that I mix in the upper circles of society and therefore many of the items I am given are valuable. Members of the Royal Family have been outstandingly generous in the past.

I was once given a genuine Aboruyu Rhino Horn snuff pouch, a present from the King of somewhere, which I sold for over £20,000. If you ever come across one of these, snap it up, they are extremely rare and, these days, would fetch something in the region of £60,000.

Likewise, anything by Arthur Maudsleydale, the 19th century inventor, some of his earlier contraptions are selling in auction for astronomical sums. And don't overlook broken Satsuma-ware, if you see a job lot of this for sale it's well worth investing. A fragmented Satsuma teapot could make you a lot of money.

Oh, and the biggest tip this month is to check our classifieds, we've added an Antiques and Collectables section. Worth a browse? I certainly think so. And remember, always sell antiques for an awful lot more than you paid for them, it's not illegal, so why not? Let *'caveat emptor'* be your motto.

<<<<<<<<>>>>>>>

Millicent 1940's Wife

War is nearly over and people throughout England are looking forward to a bright new future.

"Dwarling?" said Millicent smoothing her permanent wave efficiently. "Would you be awfully cross if I invented something called the teenager?" Millicent's husband Gordon put down his newspaper and looked at his wife querulously.

"Now Millie," he said with a kindly smile, "you simply must get these silly ideas out of your head. I know it sounds fun inventing things but it's hard work and you're unlikely to make any money. And anyway, there are the church flowers to think about and doesn't that Alice Blue Gown of yours need repairing?"

"Yes I know Dwarling." said Millicent quickly making an origami model of the Titanic out of an old ration book. "I wasn't thinking of inventing teenagers now!" she laughed, "I plan to wait until the 1950's, after all Susan and Robert will be grown up by then so I'll have more time." Gordon sighed and, polishing his Bakelite meerschaum, said, "Come on you old silly, let's not have any more talk of inventions. You've got to think about blanching that pig's head for supper and didn't I overhear you offering to sieve old Mrs. Heaton's powdered egg for her?"

Millicent bowed her head, "Yes Dwarling," she said mournfully, "but I just thought that inventing the teenager would get us out of this awful financial mess. I've thought it all through. I've got an idea for coffee bars and something I might call Rock 'n' Roll."

Gordon adjusted his monocle and stood up. His hands grasped the back of an armchair, crushing Millicent's hand-embroidered antimacassar. He was angry now.

"We went through all this when you had that soppy idea about telephones you carry around in your pocket.

Now let's just forget all about hare-brained schemes, you sit and darn your Lyle stockings, and I'll get us both an Eccles cake, shall I?"

Millicent smiled to herself. Gordon was a simply marvellous husband, "Promise you're not awfully cross Dwarling." she pleaded.

<<<<<<<<>>>>>>>>

The Egerton Review is also sponsored by:
CRAPPO-STOP
Diarrhoea Remedy

SIDE EFFECTS: *May cause Diarrhoea and Thickening and Browning of the urine and the tendency to use contradictory terminology.*

<<<<<<<<>>>>>>>>

STUFF
These are sweepings from the minds of the Commissioning Editors, ignore them if you will.

SIMPLE Mathematics for the numerically inept:

Question 1. If the hypotenuse is a chair just for boring geeky people to sit on, would you admit to being the square on it?

Multiple-choice answers:

A. I wouldn't admit to it.   B. I would admit to it.

INSTANT AMATEUR PSYCHIATRIST
JUST ADD YOUR OWN NAME to the diagnosis

Dear [INSERT NAME HERE],
So, you are feeling a bit otherworldly are you [INSERT NAME HERE]? Try not to worry too much, everyone goes through funny patches it's just that you seem to flip out more often than others.

And, if you don't mind my saying, [INSERT NAME HERE], it's unlikely that prescription drugs will help you. I don't mean to sound harsh or anything but really you are quite devoid of reason. I mean honestly, what kind of nutter dresses like that?

MIND BENDINGLY EASY CONUNDRUM

Think of the worst thing you've ever done, divide by 2, add ¾ ounce of salt and name an animal beginning with 4.

Now think of a country with the smell of ginger nut biscuits in its national anthem, multiply by 4 tons and divide by using sharp scissors. Now find the square root of any word of your choice add your date of birth and your bank balance to the total so far then subtract the amount of cigarettes you smoke from the amount of times you have farted publicly and add this figure to the name Smedley.

Multiply the sum total and divide by 3,428 and there you are!

HOW TO...
With Dalia Smythe

This month:
Reading Codes

Ascertain that what you are attempting to read is actually a code.

Decipher it and Simply read it.

<<<<<<<<>>>>>>>

The Egerton Review is also sponsored by:
Rupert Nanesque's Support Tights

SIDE EFFECTS: Irregular shaped legs, Diarrhoea and Thickening and Browning of the urine and the tendency to use contradictory terminology.

<<<<<<<<>>>>>>>

Great Put-Downs

A stranger was seated next to little Tommy on the plane when the stranger turned to the boy and said, "Let's talk, I've heard that flights will go quicker if you strike up a conversation with your fellow passengers."

Little Tommy who had just opened his book, closed it slowly, and said to the stranger, "What would you like to discuss."

"Oh, I don't know," said the stranger. "How about nuclear power?" "OK," said Little Tommy. "That would be an interesting topic but let me ask you a question first."

"A horse, a cow and a deer all eat grass, the same stuff.

Yet a deer excretes little pellets, while a cow turns out a flat patty, and a horse produces clumps of dried grass, why do you suppose that is?"

"Jeez," said the stranger. "I have no idea."

"Well then," said Little Tommy. "How is it that you feel qualified to discuss nuclear power when you don't know shit?" Little Tommy returned to his book and silence ensued.

<<<<<<<<<>>>>>>>>

In the Potting Shed with Old Nobby
A Selection of Non-Motivational Quotes from our resident miserable old git!

"All you have achieved so far, and all you have amassed is all you will achieve and amass ever. And all you have achieved so far is just a load of shit anyway!"

Letters from our Readers

The following is a selection of the boring dreary rubbish sent to us by readers of the magazine.

Dear Editors at The Egerton Review
Has anyone noticed that all your regular columnists look alike? *Mrs Winifred Freeman, Wiltshire.*
Must be a trick of the light or the highly professional level of photography. To be honest Mrs Freeman, we can't see the likeness. Sorry. The Editors

Dear Editors at The Egerton Review
Am I right in thinking that your magazine is put together by just a few very odd people as opposed to the vast staff of highly qualified columnists you claim have contributed work? *N D Milton, Hampshire.*
No, you're wrong. Sorry The Editors

Dear Editors at The Egerton Review
I don't understand your publication. Is it perhaps too intellectual for me? I have seven degrees and am a rocket scientist. *Professor Limming, Chester.*
It may well be a little over your head Professor. Sorry. The Editors

Dear Editors at The Egerton Review
Is Darcy Copperfield really a woman? *Graham Norman, Wimbledon.*
We've never asked him. Sorry The Editors

Dear Editors at The Egerton Review
I'm surprised you've printed this letter as I've never actually written to you. Am I right in thinking that you make up the letter featured on this page? *Sarah Jones, Bath.*
As if we'd do that Sarah! The Editors.

<<<<<<<<>>>>>>>>

Classified Advertisements

BOUNCY COUNCIL ESTATE
For Hire, fully insured. Inflatable entertainment you can share with others. Recommended for the aristocracy. 30-acre inflation space required. Contact: The Editors

GENUINE ARTHUR MAUDSLEYDALE Brassiere Spoon (XXXL) with spirit lamp (glass missing otherwise vgc.) No timewasters please. 12 guineas. Contact: The Editors

FOR SALE Gentle house-trained Boa Constric....
(See Obituary Column)

1 VERY CLEANLY CUT HALF of a semi dissected portion of a percentage of part of an aperture. Unwanted gift. Still in own box. (Green) 35 guineas. Contact: The Editors

VINE TOMATOES X 4 owner suddenly gone off them. 40p. Contact: The Editors.

RE-CYCLED BRINGLE-shoot shavings. Approx. 18 tons. Free to Collector. Contact: The Editors.

KING SIZE ZIP LINK with pneumatic shackle-fittings. No sensible offer entertained. Contact: The Editors.

1928 QUEUING PERISCOPE (brass and mahogany) cash or sexual favours welcomed. Contact: The Editors.

AIR GUITAR STRINGS Bass and Acoustic 6 & 12 string. Free fitting. Contact: The Editors.

<<<<<<<<>>>>>>>

PERSONAL: Man with boils wltm lady, slim and attractive with lancing tool. Enjoys cosy nights in with friendly house-trained and affectionate pet Boa Constric... (See Obituaries).

ANTIQUES AND COLLECTABLES.

Job lot of broken Satsuma-ware. A snip at £25,000. Contact D. Barrington c/o The Editors.

MISSING
1 Large Boa Constrictor

OBITUARIES

A man who had been suffering with boils was found dead in his home. His faithful, friendly Boa Constrictor, Puffles, had attempted to revive him by wrapping himself around his neck. The funeral will take place next Wednesday at Uncle Trimbles Crematorium and Children's Petting Zoo.

The casket will be open, and mourners are invited to place a single sterilized needle into the coffin. An animal expert who was called into care for the orphaned Boa Constrictor was found strangled in a flat that was once owned by a man with boils (now dead).

Police say they are baffled by the case and are looking for a random strangler with a very strong grip.

To inform us of a death, particularly involving Boa Constrictors contact us at: www.boacontrictorsstranglepeopleregularly.co.uk.gov

<<<<<<<<>>>>>>>

HUMOUR FROM THE 19th CENTURY
"Why should the number 288 never be mentioned in company? Because it is two gross."

<<<<<<<<>>>>>>>

The Egerton Review

Things you never wanted to know, told to you by people who know nothing about them

Vol. 1   February 2004

Our Chairman, self-made Bringle-Shoot hemp millionaire, Stet (Chubby) Chetson, showing he can point with both hands.

RANCH SELLING IN TEXAS – THE PITFALLS

Last month we brought you news that Stet Chetson intended to invest money in our esteemed publication. Well, he hasn't sold the ranch yet so don't expect any four-colour separation just yet.

He informs us that one of the problems of selling his ranch is that everybody in Texas already owns one and finding someone who doesn't own one and wants to buy one is very slim (unlike Stet (Fatty) Chetson).

We believe the main reason for his inability to sell his ranch is that he doesn't bloody well own one!

Stet is now embarked on a tour of the UK which seems a safe enough bet as a quick money spinner seeing as there are still quite a few people who haven't yet realised he's not an American. Stet's album, 'Big Ranchman Sings Country' is terrible so don't bother with it.

Anyway, it's Issue Two time already, no sooner had we spent the money we got for Issue one, that we had to hock the TV to prepare another scintillating edition of our hilarious magazine.

I suppose, as it is now February you are expecting fluffy Valentine's wishes, well don't, we can't be bothered with all that smarmy rubbish.

Well, you are probably thinking, or not, as the case maybe, what wonders have we got for you this time? You will remember that our very own Lord Beauderriere is planning to release a biography of the Countess de Verucca.

The Countess is more than a little miffed about this. Support for both parties has been pouring into our offices and although we couldn't print all of the letters, we will be bringing the more colourful epistles to you.

Darcy Copperfield brings you another insight into the world of erotic literature and Kev Mugton's daughter Tracy, has got herself a man, well Lord Beauderriere's son Timothy, actually, so we'll be following that catastrophe to its conclusion.

We'll have the usual load of old tripe, and we are still waiting for your contributions, so get a move on.

<<<<<<<<>>>>>>>
Funny Bits

The reason why the Lone Ranger shot Tonto is because he found out that Kemo Sabe meant 'Flash Prick'

<<<<<<<<>>>>>>>

I feel we must take a moment to congratulate ourselves, the Editors I mean, on having produced yet another monthly issue of this fantastic outstanding magazine (our words). To be honest I never thought we'd get this far. It shows that with grit, expertise and mental acumen you can achieve anything, that and a gullible readership!

Darcy Copperfield's
Literature Unleashed

At the tender age of ten Darcy Copperfield was expelled from St. Peregrine's School for Boys for writing 'Anne of Green Gables is a nymphomaniac' on the blackboard. How times have changed, nowadays Copperfield's observations about sex and perversion in literature are respected and salivated over worldwide.

Jane Eyre Unbuttoned

It is a truth universally acknowledged that Jane Eyre is probably one of the most misunderstood writers of all time. People, even those you'd think would know better, constantly muddle her up with Fanny Burney, or think, wrongly I must stress, that she wrote Middlemarch and was a man. Jane Eyre is the supposedly prim little genius who wrote the famous frock frolic in which the snobby Heathcliff gets, eventually, to marry Elizabeth. But where's your sex? There's plenty of it I can assure you.

When the Vicar of Ambridge points out that Lady Catherine Deneuve of Rosings Park has several staircases he's doing it to let the reader know that Heathcliff will be hotfooting it up one of them to get to Miss Bennet's boudoir.

By that time, he's already smitten with the comely country girl and has, no doubt, already dallied with her day bonnet on more than one occasion. Remember how he said her eyes were brightened by exercise? Well, how could he know?

And what form of exercise does the eminent Mr Heathcliff, of Wildfell Hall, enjoy? Put it this way, he's not described as proud and upright for nothing. Need I say more? Not really but I will. Heathcliff is clearly not the innocent we like to think him, after all, he's got a mad wife locked away in the attic. What turned her crazy I'd like to know?

And how does he pay Grace Poole? There's never any mention of her getting her wages and it's Eyre's omission of the facts that leads me to deduce that Grace was in receipt of much more than a handful of thru'pennies. An erotic book? If you take out all the 'Pray tell me's' and substitute the phrase 'afternoon tea' with a 'good hard humping' it most certainly is. **My erotica rating is XXX**

COULD YOU WRITE EROTIC FICTION?
Send your exotic fantasies, in the form of a short story, to Darcy Copperfield c/o The Egerton Review for use in any other edition of the Review or for Darcy's personal files. Please include a photograph of yourself. Sorry we can't return submissions.

We honestly believe that Darcy has never picked up, let alone read, a book in his entire life. The Commissioning Editors.

<<<<<<<<<>>>>>>>>

...The End
the end of a clichéd story for those who can't be bothered to read a whole book.

We have all looked at and picked up a book thinking that's interesting, thumbed through it and then put it down and perhaps later wished you had read it. Here is a book you may have done that to précised here for your convenience.

Frigid Jones' Diary
By Helen Fieldmouse

Story so far: *Frigid Jones, a dairy worker who hasn't got a boyfriend, decides to document the plight of her sex in diary format. Jones, who believes she is overweight (but-clearly-isn't-really-given-that-she-is-portrayed-by-someone-quite-slim-in-the-feature-film-of-the-book) has just been ditched by neighbouring butcher-cum-stud Daniel Meatcleaver because his sexual needs outweighed her own.*

Frigid is just beginning to realise that apparently boring Mark D'Arsehole, a lifelong acquaintance, is a more than nice man who she has been being rude to throughout the book.

Will Frigid finally peel off her great big milkmaid's bloomers and jump into D'Arsehole's paddling pool?...

Monday
Saw Mark D'Arsehole at the Annual Churning Fete. Have not forgiven him for beating up Daniel Meatcleaver in the Pig's Trotter the other night. Wanker. I am immensely fat and incapable of getting a boyfriend.

Cigarettes: 0 - don't smoke am clean living country lass.
Alcohol: 0 - don't drink unless you count sherry at Christmas which disagreed with me and was probably responsible for Uncle T having his way with me under the mistletoe.
Butter: 24 tons - hand churned and dispatched to Anchor headquarters this morning.

Tuesday: Saw Mark D'Arsehole at agricultural fair. Felt left out. Only singleton there. Everyone else was clever and accompanied by a prize pig or some such companion. Mark v kind. Offered to drive me home in Land Rover. Probably wanted sex.

Wednesday : Mark D'Arsehole did want sex. Said no. Am still frigid. Best friend Wazza say am mad as Mark D'Arsehole is image of famous actor called Colin, who, apparently, is highly desirable. Wouldn't know or care, haven't got a telly. Keep trying to remind people that I am frigid.

Thursday: Just been reminded that once frolicked naked in Mark D'Arsehole's paddling pool. Can't believe it.
Am probably sex maniac who enjoys shagging to having a proper boyfriend.

Friday: Dressed up as dominatrix for local garden party. Chased Mark D'Arsehole through village, finally catching up with him outside the church. Got married. Ahh.
   Am really marvellous girl who everyone thought was pretending to be frigid and lacking in confidence...**The End.**

<<<<<<<<<>>>>>>>

Neville Slipton's
Language Workshop
"My tongue is my passport."

Neville Slipton was born Susan Grace Sliptonova in 1956. His mother was French/Indonesian, and his father was Russian. His deep interest in, and unrivalled grasp of, languages stemmed from living in a multi-lingual environment in no less than forty-three countries.

Panting For It

Hi, it occurred to me, as I sauntered flamboyantly through the piazza last week that communication with the humble natives, although easy for a smooth tongued bon vivuer like myself, can prove difficult for those whose experience of travel is limited.

For example, as I sat in the street café. The foam from my French chocolat chaud frothing delectably on my lips I noticed an English person trying to tell the lithe, olive-skinned waiter that he desired a plate of egg and chips.

Quelle disaster! The Englishman, an insult to an Italian suit if there ever was one, was getting nowhere and yet with a wink, a smile, and a quick massage of the waiter's hurt Gefuhle I managed to procure the aforementioned platter of eouf & frites without so much as raising my voice.

A miracle? Not at all, just a question of adopting the simpatico attitudes of the indigenes and learning a few simple to understand phrases. I find it helps to carry a gentleman's handbag when abroad and, if you really want to fit in with immaculately dressed and handsome young Latinos, wear tight buff coloured trousers, remembering never put the keys to your Alfa-Romero in your pocket. It ruins the cut of the cloth and distorts the otherwise impressive taglio del vostro fiocco.

So, remember, *tight pants and a smooth tongue. Viola! This month's phrase is:*

In English: *"Excuse me, handsome young subservient being with thighs of astonishing firmness, kindly bring me some regional delicacies and other morsels."*

In French: *Excusez-moi, jeune être subservient beau avec des cuisses de la fermeté étonnate, apportez-avec bonté moi quelques délicatesses régionales et d'autres morsels.*

In German: *Entschuldigen Sie mich stattliches junges subservient Sein mit Schenkeln de erstaunlichen Festigkeit holen Sie mir irgendeine regionale Zartheit und andere morcelgruebershcnitzel freundlich.*

In Italian: *Scusilo essere subservient giovane belle con le coscie fermezze astonishing gentilmente portimi alcune squisitezze regionali ed altri morcelli.*

<<<<<<<<<>>>>>>>>

at home with...
The Beauderriere's

Lord Beauderriere, in his ignorance, believes that the general viewing public is chomping at the bit to hear of the exploits of this dissolute excuse for an aristocrat. To our eyes, it's just a feeble ruse to relive his salad days. He prefers to use this picture of himself. We don't know why, nor do we care, as any picture of him now would scare the horses and small children

A SCRIPT FOR TELEVISION

EPISODE 2: LORD BEAUDERRIERE, A KINDLY MASTER

SCENE 1 (IN WHICH LORD BEAUDERRIERE IS FIRM BUT GENTLE

CAST: LORD B - AN ARISTOCRAT
        BIMSY SNEDWELL - A YOUNG MAN

INT: LORD BEAUDERRIERE IS SITTING, HIS BUTTOCKS STRAINING, IN A TATTERED WICKER CHAIR.

LORD BEAUDERRIERE
I say Bimsy, once you've finished greasing the elephant gun, I shall allow you to sit upon my knee.

BIMSY
No way.

LORD BEAUDERRIERE
I'm very rich and important you snivelling prat. Now get your backside down here or I'll report you to the High Commissioner of Bututangi

BIMSY
Is there something wrong with you?

LORD BEAUDERRIERE
Come a bit closer and I'll tell you.

In the next issue Lord Beauderriere chats to his Butler

<<<<<<<<>>>>>>>

Countess de Verucca's
Liquid Lunch

The Countess has failed to provide a brief biography for our readers' benefit. We apologise for the appalling transcript, but the Countess gave us her column early one morning on our rather old answering machine, we have done our best.

Boozing Before Breakfast

Duis autem vel eum iriure dolor in hendrerit in vulputate esse consequat, vel illum dolore eu feugiat nulla facilisis at very pissed eros et accumsan et hendrerit in vulputate velit esse molestie consequat. Vel illum room null aiusto odio dig Brandy nissum.

Duis autem vel eum iriure dolore in hendrerit in vulputate velit esse consequat, vel Duis autem vel eum iriure dolor in hendrerit in vulputate esse make that a double consequat, vel illum brandy dolore eu feugiat nulla facilisis eros et accumsan et hendrerit in vulputate velit esse molestie consequat. Vel illum null aiusto odio dig nissum. Duis Shiraz autem vel eum iriure sed diam nonummy dolore in drunk hendrerit Vel illum null Bacardi Breezer aiusto odio dig nissum. Duis autem vel eum iriure dolore in hendrerit in vulputate Cabernet Sauvignon, Claret velit esse and a bottle of Famous Grouse consequat, vel ex ea.

Duis autem vel eum iriure head was spinning around and around dolor in hendrerit in vulputate esse consequat, vel illum dolore eu feugiat. Duis autem in a Cocktail Bar vel eum iriure dolor in hendrerit in vulputate Gin and Tonic, Baileys, and a large glass of Harvey's Bristol Cream esse consequat, vel illum dolore eu surprised feugiat nulla facilisis taken from behind eros et accumsan et Hungarian Weightlifter.

Hendrerit in vulputate velit esse molestie consequat. nulla facilisis eros et accumsan et hendrerit in Bacardi Breezer vulputate velit esse molestie consequat. Vel illum ar null aiusto odio dig nissum. Duis autem vel smashed offa my face eum iriure dolore in Cabernet Sauvignon. Duis autem vel eum iriure dolor in hendrerit in vulputate esse consequat, vel illum dolore eu feugiat nulla facilisis at very pissed eros et accumsan et hendrerit in vulputate velit esse molestie consequat. hendrerit pissed outa my brains.

<<<<<<<<<>>>>>>>>

'Zen' Sven's
Sphere of Enigma

Note for readers. Unlike our other columnists 'Zen' Sven declined to be photographed. He believes that a visual image of him might detract from the serious and fascinating nature of his column, we actually believe it is because he is so devastatingly ugly that no one would ever believe a word he says.

WEIRD CREATURES
Astonishing accounts of Demi-Gonks living in rural England

Forget the Beast of Bodmin Moor. Put the Loch Ness Monstrosity out of your mind. Don't even think about the Phoenix or Puff the Magic Dragon. Erase all knowledge of the Jabberwocky and every other mythical creature.

They are but nothing when compared to the outlandish beasts that roam the peaceful pastures of this green and pleasant land. I went to meet Hector Hockett, a pig-swill processor from Hertfordshire who was amongst the first to spot what is being called a Demi-Gonk in a barn not far from his home.

"I was completely stunned," says Hector, who was recently released into the community. "The creature had the head and body of a human but the facial features, hair and demeanour of a Gonk."

Mrs Betty Oates, another local who is recovering from a lobotomy when I meet her, reports,

"I first saw the Demi-Gonk last month; I'd just come out of hospital the day I saw it. It walked into my garden carrying a can of Special Brew, growled at me and then slunk off behind the potting shed. We think it's been eating the chickens."

So, is there any evidence to suggest that Demi-Gonks actually exist? Luckily, another local person was able to capture an image of a Demi-Gonk on camera

"It just stood there, swaying and it seemed quite happy to pose for a photo. I couldn't believe it." says Wilf Citanul. "The strange thing was that I didn't feel afraid.

At first, I thought it was my daughter-in-law who is a strippagram, then I realised it was fully clothed and had a better figure than her." With such sound testimonies from so many reliable witnesses I can only conclude that Demi-Gonks really do exist.

This is believed to be the first image of a Demi-Gonk in the wild.

Ye Olde Advertisement for your Delectation
The Most Sovereign Contraption Introduced for The Comfort of Ladies

Arthur Maudsleydale's Brassiere Spoon

Wonderful and most Excellent for scooping and securing a maiden's ripeness. Especially Designed for the well-endowed lady. Cures Flushes and overspill of the Cups instantly.

This most excellent equipage comes with Spoon, Spirit Lamp and Spoon Rest

<<<<<<<<>>>>>>>

Dr. Makitupp Azugoalong's
Quick Clinic

All too aware that medical jargon and detailed diagnoses can worry patients, Dr Azugoalong, an avid Iron Maiden fan, set up the first on-line Monosyllabic Medical Response Clinic in 1998.. Dr Azugoalong speaks very little English.

Dear Doctor Azugoalong
When I consulted you about an ear, nose and throat problem you told me to strip off. My husband has since found out and says that your behaviour was unethical. He has no medical experience, and I wonder if he's being over cautious. Is he?
Yes.

Dear Doctor Azugoalong
Thank you for taking so much trouble over my recent clitoral realignment therapy. You seemed so dedicated and attentive that I wanted to write and let other potential patients know. My sister-in-law, Beryl, who is frigid, says that you are completely out of order and ought to be struck off. I think she's jealous, don't you?
Yes.

Dear Doctor Azugoalong
I recently approached my GP about having an affair with me. He said it would be against his principles. Are all Drs so cautious and correct?
No.

Dear Doctor Azugoalong
I'm sure I once bought a packet of mango scented joss sticks from you while holidaying in what was then Ceylon. Was it you? I'm not sure now. Is my memory totally mangled by the constant use of drugs?
Yes.

Dear Doctor Azugoalong
You know I said I would meet you behind the autoclave next week? Well, I can't now because I've got to take our budgie to be put down. Would Tuesday be all right and could the venue be the surgical waste troughs?

Yes.

Always remember, Dr Azugoalong is <u>NOT</u> an Aromatherapist as he suffers from Anosmia* and is in it just for the money. *Anosmia – No sense of smell.

<<<<<<<<>>>>>>>

Public Eye
your observations appreciated
doppelgangers
We invite you to send in examples of look-alikes. Only the most astounding resemblances will be published.

Dora Remington observes.
My son, Theodore is the spitting image of a man I met in Swindon, or was it Sweden? Anyway, if any of your readers know someone from Sweden or Swindon that looks like my son, they will be amazed too. What do the readers think?

children say the funniest things
C'mon you little gits, say something funny!!
How we didn't laugh!

<<<<<<<<>>>>>>>

Witty Man
He's got an answer for every occasion

"??????????????"

Sorry, Witty Man isn't as funny as we thought. Therefore, we are unable to print anything he has said in the last month as it has been meaningless shite. We've taken away his picture, we shall take away his salary next!

<<<<<<<<<>>>>>>>

The Beauderriere/de Verucca Kerfuffle

Lord

Beauderriere, on whom our script for television is based, announced last month that he has written, and intends to publish, a biography of The Countess de Verucca, our very own wines and spirits connoisseur. Beauderriere's book, an unauthorised account of the Countess's life, has caused uproar amongst the upper echelons of Italian society. The Countess herself asked us to print her letter last month, this month her solicitor writes:

Hanns, Neece & Boompadasey
10307 Extortion House Legal Lane London W1

Lord Beauderriere
Hotel Bastado

My Lord (*hereafter referred to as 'that bastard'*)

I am instructed by my client, (*hereafter referred to as 'my client'*) the Countess de Verucca, to give you formal notification that the publication of your forthcoming biography **'The Uncensored Verucca,'** (*hereafter called 'that crap book'*) will not be welcomed by my client and that my client hereby denies that there is any truth in any of the content contained therein.

I will henceforth, on the instruction of my client, issue forthwith a legal document thereby outlining the legalities of this matter and hereby propose to commence immediate legal action against you which, in the light of the situation, will be delayed for a period not exceeding fourteen days and no less than four days.

Provided that the above specifications are adhered to in full, without exception and in a manner thereby outlined in the lay-by. Notwithstanding full responsibility for the outcome of any omissions you may have deliberately made to favour the contrafibularities of the logistical impact, either probable or calculated in the light of unmeritorious solicitations, I think.

In closing, I should further suggest that our client, the prestigious and virtually flawless Countess, has been the subject of this kind of literary calumny before. The fact that the books have never been published and that the authors are living out a squalid existence in the most unsavoury part of Milton Keynes leads me to surmise that a letter of total retraction is heading out way from yourself.

In closing, I should like to suggest that the overall concept of your book, i.e. that the Countess is a 'flatulent, alcoholic, narcissistic old tart and let us prove it in print' is particularly alarming, considering its accuracy. Such accuracy achieves nothing, particularly in a court of law. In closing, we say 'ready for the scrum down.' Please feel free to enter into written exchanges with us, we charge the Countess an exorbitant fee for these letters. *Yours sincerely, Jeremiah Hanns*

More to come...perhaps.

<<<<<<<<>>>>>>>

Funny Bits
Went to see a psychic. I knocked on her door.
She called out "Who is it?" So, I Left!

<<<<<<<<<>>>>>>>

Rick Faberge's Column
"Even some thing's I don't like are expensive"

Rick Faberge shot to fame as lead singer of the 70's rock band 'Superstud Megastar'. He owns a castle in Scotland and collects expensive things. He has been married nine times to six different blondes. Rick enjoys spending money and having sex. Sometimes the two enjoyments have had to be combined.

Tasteful—Tacky?
Is there a difference? Rick Faberge investigates

Being a multi-billionaire means that my homes are strewn with tasteful objects. I guess I'm lucky to have an eye for what works and what doesn't. But it isn't just about money. It's about style. I was trying to explain the difference between tasteful and tacky to my girlfriend, Anouskana, the other day but there wasn't much point.

She's had a little too much bubbly the night before and wasn't listening. But for the benefit of those of you who haven't been drinking Timotei I will explain. So: Tasteful? Tacky? *Is* there a difference. If you can't tell then you're probably the tacky sort. Test yourself. Have all the women you know got fingernails with very white square ends? If yes, then you've got taste. You can spot tasteful people in many ways; their all year round tans are a big clue for starters.

And the addition of leopard-skin to the bedroom is a subtle indicator of a stylish and tasteful person. Tacky people simply turn their noses up at some of the black ash effect furniture on the market these days preferring dusty old stuff that should have been chucked out years ago. In my Spanish villa I've gone for the minimalist look. Just one padded vinyl mini bar and waterbed per room. No need to overdo it.

That would be tacky. Likewise, to many gilded gargoyles, I just have the one musical Elvis water-feature and statuette in the hallway which adds impact. Briefly, anything made of natural materials screams tacky and should be avoided.

<<<<<<<<>>>>>>>

Hollywood Interviews

Each Month one of our Columnists will interview a famous Hollywood Star. This month Neville Slipton talks to Troy Blushe, avant-garde director of such films as I Was A Teenage Teenager; Teenage Lovers; Teenage Lovers—The Early Years.

Neville: Well Troy, quelle mange! It's really lovely to meet you.

Troy: It's great to be here, and to talk about my new...

Neville: Yes, of course, but you're early work, mostly teenagers, how was that?

Troy: Well, it was great working with young raw talent.

Neville: Mmm, all those young people in skimpy clothes, their long hair blowing in the wind...

Troy: Oh yes, the young girls were really lovely.

Neville: Oh, you had girls as well, I didn't know that.

Troy: Yes, some of them went on to become quite established stars.

Neville: Yeah, great. who was your favourite young man?

Troy: Well, I didn't really have a favourite, they were all very good.

Neville: Place de la Concorde! You had them all!!

Troy: Well, yes, I gave them all a position...

Neville: I bet...what fun, I think one ought to try all the positions too!

Troy: You seem to be putting a sexual leaning to this interview... there was nothing like that at all.

Neville: Nothing, oh well.

At this point Neville lost interest in the interview and after a while left the room.

<<<<<<<<>>>>>>>

It has just come to our notice that the Hollywood Interviews are just a vehicle for our columnist to talk about themselves or steer the conversation into unseemly areas. That's all, it just came to our notice.

<<<<<<<<>>>>>>>

Kev Mugton's
Fine Art Course

Kev Mugton shot to fame after a brief appearance on TV when he famously miscut some MDF and emulsioned a 17th century marble fireplace. Kev has always been interested in painting but has no experience whatsoever. Kev hopes to win the Mastermind Rose Bowl too but that's unlikely as he is fundamentally thick as two miscut planks.

Sculpture for Everyone

Allo, Now, I don't know about you, but I couldn't be bothered to carve a woman out of marble. If you want something to stand in your lounge then you can buy these moulds from craft shops. You just pour in Plaster of Paris, wait for it to dry and that's it.

You'd have to be wrong in the head to spend half your life tackling David's bollocks with a chisel. If you like something a bit more modern then you could build a wonky brick wall, shit on the top of it and glue a tin of beans to the side.

Between you and me that's what I'm entering for next year's Turner Prize. I knocked it up last week round me Nan's. She reckons the beans'll have gone off by then. That'll just add to the value in my opinion.

Right then, sculpting. Sculpting is when you make something out of something else. Like when you get a knife and carve out Kev woz 'ere in an old tree.

That's the sort of idea of sculpting only it's not quite the same cos if it was sculpting what you'd do would be get a big lump of wood and carve it into a tree and *then* carve Kev woz 'ere into it.

Actually, you wouldn't carve Kev woz 'ere into it if you're name was Baz or something else so try to remember that. Oh, and the other thing is that if you sculpt things then you are a sculptist. A bit like if you paint things you are a paintist. No that isn't right is it? No, I always mix them up.

Anyway, people are always asking me what sort of art I have in my house. Well, most of the stuff I've got is my own work, original Mugtons if you like. I did a picture last week with glitter glue.

It's of this Spanish Lady. I done the castanets in red.

<<<<<<<<<>>>>>>>

Marjorie Kyte-Hopper's
Guide to Life

Marjorie Kyte-Hopper's career as Advisor to the World began when, as a Brownie, she started bossing people about and giving her opinions freely. Marjorie, who was married only once, briefly married, recently published a book, 'Country Looks for the Woolly-Haired.'

She lives in Norfolk with her dog Attila. Marjorie, much to her astonishment, is a gay icon

Taking Drugs

Hello Dear Readers, every Wednesday a Drug Advice Group meets in my local Village Hall. I'm astonished by this I must say because most drugs these days come with detailed instructions as to how they should be used.

For example, the leaflet included with my migraine tablets is self-explanatory. Take two pink ones at the onset of an attack and a yellow one in the midst of an attack. it couldn't be simpler. So why the need for a Drug Advice group in our sleepy village? I went along to find out. I was astounded to see so many unhealthy people there. It really brought the message home I can tell you.

None of the attendants looked as if they could even manage to get the lid off of a bottle of aspirin let alone read the instructions. I immediately changed my tune and decided that the Drug Advice Group was a good thing.

As I was there, I took the time to talk to many of the people and can safely say they went away looking absolutely amazed. It seems that they were so stunned by what I had to tell them that they no longer feel the need to attend the group.

One of them said to me, "It's a waste of sodding time coming here." Isn't that marvellous? I was so happy to be able to help with what is such an easy to solve problem. If you think you have a problem with drugs take the time to read the leaflet and everything will turn out fine.

Finally, it's nothing to be ashamed of, lots of lovely people have difficulty following instructions.

I learned at the Drug Advice Group that many young people enjoy speed. I don't understand why doing things fast was being talked about at such a group, but my advice is that if you like freewheeling on your bicycle or sprinting that's your choice and it's nothing to worry about at all.

<<<<<<<<>>>>>>>

Funny Bits
The police turned up last night and said my dogs were chasing kids on bikes. Bit surprised, my dogs don't have bikes!

<<<<<<<<>>>>>>>

Vitally Important Psychological Test

Since the first issue was released, we've had letters from readers who have become concerned about their mental wellbeing and ours. The last thing we want to do is to drive our readers insane.

In order to reassure yourselves that you haven't gone crazy, we have, with the help of Dr Azugoalong who is **NOT** an aromatherapist, devised a simple, yet absolutely valid multiple choice self-testing psychological system.

Before taking the test ensure that you have read Marjorie Kyte Hopper's column in a public place. A crowded train or busy London street is ideal.

Keep calm at all times and when you feel confident gently insert one finger in your left ear and the other in the left ear of the person next to you. Say *'I am not from outer-space I am merely a reader of The Egerton Review.'* in a clear voice, preferably adopting a Swedish accent (not essential).

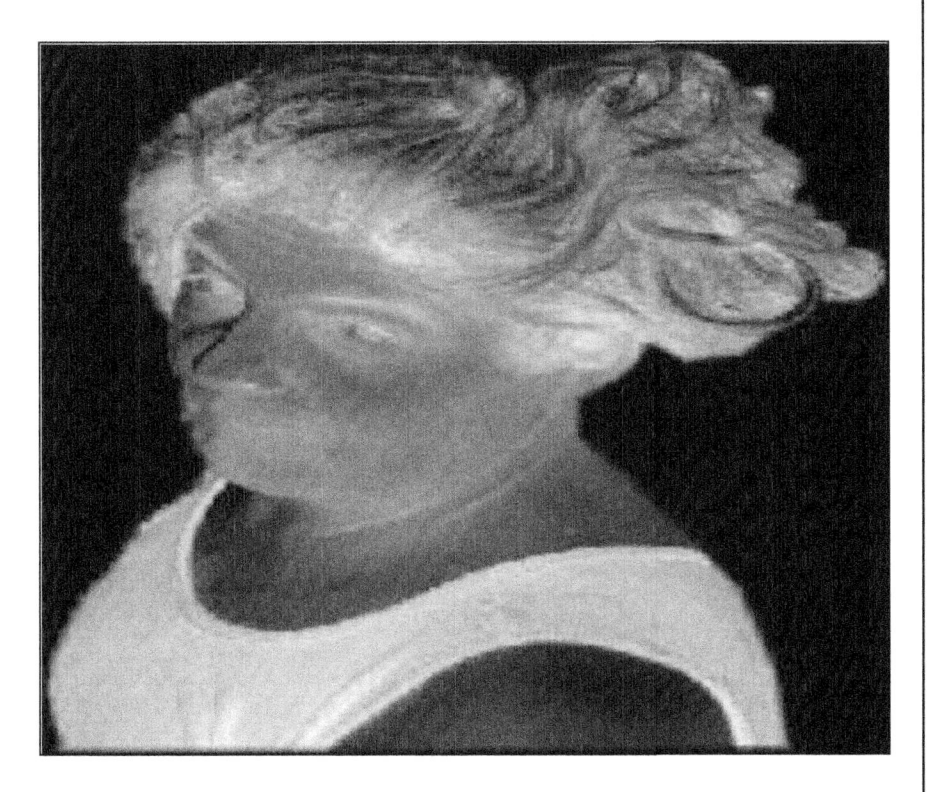

Then place your nose onto the image above. Breathe deeply while singing an old sea-shanty then whisk the page away from you keeping it at arm's length for the next 20 seconds.

Finally, go cross-eyed and the image above should have become clear. Using our multiple choice section, select the description which most suits the image you thought you saw.

Psychological analysis is included with each answer.

I thought I saw two people face to face but then I got confused and thought it was a vase.
(WRONG, YOU MUST BE MAD)

I thought I saw a horse with no name.
(WRONG, YOU MUST BE MAD)

I taught I taw- a - puddy-cat. I did, I taw- a- puddy-cat.
(WRONG, YOU MUST BE MAD)

69

I thought I saw someone trying to get my finger out of their ear, but then I looked at the picture.
(WRONG, YOU MUST BE MAD)

I thought I saw through your stupid psychological test, which I initially believed was a trick devised to make me look like an imbecile, but then I went ahead with it.
(WRONG, YOU MUST BE MAD)

I thought I saw the Virgin Mary in a tin of beans? Am I right? (NO, AND THAT SUBJECT WAS COVERED EXTENSIVELY IN OUR LAST ISSUE. YOU MUST BE MAD)

I thought I saw one of your columnists but I'm not sure which one...Is it Darcy Copperfield
(NO, YOU'RE WRONG, YOU MUST BE MAD)

I thought saw Auntie Marjorie but as I had read the article and followed the instructions, I feel that this is impossible.
(NO, YOU'RE WRONG, YOU MUST BE MAD)

<<<<<<<<>>>>>>>

Text Message From History
I overheard this conversation in the Space Lunar module just before it took off for earth, "No, Neil, you did not give me the ignition key".

<<<<<<<<>>>>>>>

Dorset Barrington's
Antique Dealing

Dorset Barrington's interest in becoming an antique dealer was inflamed by the vast amount of profit he made from selling off various priceless family heirlooms as a child.

Collector's Codpiece

When I was a young man, I stumbled upon one of our servants using a rather rusty Arthur Maudsleydale Brassiere Spoon. Since then, I have been fascinated, not only by Arthur Maudsleydale, the famous 19th Century Innovator, but by servants, rust *and* breasts. Arthur Maudsleydale was responsible for such delights as the Gonad Balconette, the Clitoral Klaxon and the Clockwork Flap Smoother.

All items which, I am sure you agree, changed the face of history and the faces of the users. Genuine Maudsleydale Innovations are, today, highly prized, highly priced and highly desirable. A little bit like me!

I've been a collector of Maudsleydalia for many years now and my library houses many stunning examples of the rarer pieces. It is unusual to come across mint condition Maudsleydalia, there is usually some degree of restoration required although I would urge collectors to try to maintain the objects' original finishing where possible.

For example, most Brassiere Spoons show corrosion to the brass links and the leather shackling found on most boudoir accoutrements will need extensive lubricating. Replacing components of Maudsleydale items can be tricky. Although they were built to the highest specification the more intricate mechanisms often suffer from Verdigris markings and seizure. A light oiling will free off any stubborn thigh clamps or anal gussets. So, what are Maudsleydale items worth today? A bloody fortune.

Even pieces in poor condition fetch a pretty price, in fact, with the Genitalia range, a play-worn appearance and friction marks are sought after.

<<<<<<<<>>>>>>>

Millicent 1940's Wife

War is nearly over and people throughout England are looking forward to a bright new future.

"Dwarling?" said Millicent rinsing her Oxo tin confidently. "Would you be *awfully* cross if I invented something called the Personal Computer?" Millicent's husband Gordon toyed with the keys to his potting shed and looked at his wife nervously.

"Now Millington-poopsy," he said with a kindly nod of his head, "you simply must get these silly ideas out of your head. You invent something new every month and quite frankly I find it disturbing. And anyway, there's that doodlebug to polish and weren't you supposed to be entertaining Mrs Hartlepool's American friend this afternoon?" "Yes I know Dwarling." said Millicent deftly producing a batch of fresh Spam fritters for the W.I. fete." I wasn't thinking of inventing the personal computer now!" she laughed,

"I plan to wait until the late 1980's, Susan and Robert will be of retirement age and living away from home by then, so I'll have more time." Gordon sighed and, buffing his gramophone aggressively, said, "Come on old horse, let's not have any more talk of inventions. You've got to think about making some pigs foot jelly and didn't I overhear you offering to throw a street party for the orphans? Millicent cast her eyes downward, "Yes Dwarling," she said sorrowfully, "but I just thought that inventing the personal computer would get us out of this dreadful financial mess. I've thought it all through, simply everyone would have one by the year 2003.

Gordon removed his bicycle clips and thrust his hands deeply into his trouser pockets and idly fingered his dibber. He was furious now. "We went through all this when you had that lame idea about cloning sheep. Now let's just forget all about cloud cuckoo land ideas, you sit and hold my dibber, and I'll get us both a lovely cup of Horlicks, shall

> *You haven't been having ideas again have you poppet?*
>
> *Only silly ones that would probably make us rich Dwarling.*

I?" Millicent smiled to herself. Gordon was the most divine husband in the world. "Promise you're not *awfully* cross Dwarling." she pleaded.

<<<<<<<<>>>>>>>

The Egerton Review is also sponsored by:
Nurse Bloom's Groin Strengthening Elastic Pants
Not recommended for anyone with a weakness in the groinal area
Side Effects: Groin Weakness, bruising, , Irregular shaped legs, Diarrhoea and Thickening and Browning of the urine and the tendency to use contradictory terminology.

<<<<<<<<>>>>>>>

Slightly Mutated Foreign Phrases
By changing just one letter, foreign words and phrases take on new meanings

Entrepreneuf: Come in number nine.

Cafeat emptor: Coffee buyer beware.

Decree Nice: That ridiculous phase of a divorce when both parties believe (wrongly) that things can be worked out amicably.

Degas Vous: A Strange experience of thinking you've seen an artist's work before.

Virilante: A sexually vengeful person.

Vindalog: Heavy faeces produced after consumption of fierce curry.

Nom de Plum: A false but fruity name.

Pseudogym: Term applied to the practice of adopting the identity of one who regularly exercises.

Announcement

I hear a trumpet fanfare in my head, but not in my heart...the following is going to be a disaster.

<<<<<<<<<>>>>>>>>

The Mugton/Short-Cummings Wedding Announcement

The Editors are somewhat numbed to announce the forthcoming nuptials of Timothy Short-Cummings, son and heir to the impressive Beauderriere debts, and Tracey Mugton, daughter of Kev Mugton, art critic and jobbing builder.

The Short-Cummings-Mugton union is one which comes as no surprise to friends of Short-Cummings who say that Timothy, who was a virgin until last week, has fallen head over heels in love with the raunchy (and slightly tarty) Miss Mugton.

The Bride-to-be, who is training to be a hair and beauty specialist, appears to be equally smitten with the recently de-flowered son of a lord.

"'I thought 'e was a right git at first and some of me mates reckoned he was a bit of a tosser because he ain't got a chin. But I told 'em he had a huge lot of cash and they quite like him now."

Miss Mugton, who clearly never reads the papers and therefore has no concept of the financial shit most of the aristocracy are now obliged to wade through, agreed to marry Mr Short-Cummings after he proposed to her in the grounds of Beauderriere Castle.

Lord Beauderriere, who spoke to us from the confines of his tattered wicker chair, said last night,

"Fwah, fwah, fwah, fwah, phoar, good childbearing hips, boobs to kill for and an arse like a good pig. Jolly good show. Looking forward to breaking her in." The wedding is to take place within the next few months and will be solemnized at the private chapel (St Wayne's & St Sharon's) at Beauderriere Castle.

The bridal gown is being designed by Gerald Melton, funeral parlour make-up artiste and dress designer. We know that Mr. Melton can make the dead look attractive, but we are not sure how he will deal with the dead common. We can report that Nigel Dodson Harcourt-

Jones, lifelong friend and confidante of Timothy Short-Cummings will be best man. The bride's maid of honour will be Kylie Shanks, described rather typically, as one of Tracey's 'best mates.'

No society wedding would be complete without interference from a well-known publication. However, no well-known publications have shown any interest in interfering with the Short-Cummings-Mugton wedding so it's down to The Egerton Review to take intrusive photographs of the bride swilling rum and black down her neck.

From that you will surmise that we will be covering what is being called the wedding of the century, in our esteemed publication. Look out for our special edition soon. We will more than likely not bother but hey, who cares!

<<<<<<<<>>>>>>>

In the Potting Shed with Old Nobby
A Selection of Non-Motivational Quotes from our resident miserable old git!

"If at first you don't succeed, it's probably because it's never going to happen!"

<<<<<<<<>>>>>>>

Letters from our Readers
The following is a selection of the boring dreary rubbish sent to us by readers of the magazine.

Dear Editors at The Egerton Review,
I'd like to get in touch with my feminine side but haven't seen it for many years. I lost touch with it when I decided to become a really macho body builder. If anyone has seen my feminine side (last thought to be living in the Stoke Newington area) please could they contact me.
Dan Graves.
We would gladly encourage our readers to contact you Dan but unfortunately you forgot to state what mental institution you are writing from. Sorry. The Editors

Dear Editors at The Egerton Review,
I quite fancy Rick Faberge but understand he only goes for blondes. Is it worth me dyeing my hair?
Ingrid Boobssen. P.S I'm not Swedish, will that matter?
Rick is already happily having several affairs. Don't think he'd be able to fit you in love. Sorry. The Editors

Dear Editors at The Egerton Review,
I was disturbed by the death of a boa constrictor lover reported in last month's issue Most animals, even those thought to be violent are really friendly once you get to know them. I recently bought a large boa constric....
See Obituaries The Editors

Dear Editors at The Egerton Review
I'm positive that Dr Azugoalong lives on my estate. If it is him, I'm surprised, given his status, that he can't afford to buy his own house and that he signs on the dole. I would write to him directly, but I was put off because
I thought he'd probably give me a one-word answer to this query. Can you throw any light onto the matter?
Beryl Nosey
No. The Editors

Dear Editors at The Egerton Review,
Are you all out of your sodding minds?
A Well-Wisher
Yes. Sorry. The Editors

You know we won't answer letters personally so stop sending SAE's, invitations to tea or the boring orgies you keep planning. We're not interested.

<<<<<<<<>>>>>>>

Obituaries

A woman was found dead in her home. Police say that she was probably the victim of a serial killer. Her pet boa-constrictor, who was obviously trying to revive her, was wound tightly around her neck. The woman died whilst writing a letter to The Egerton Review. The funeral will take place at the Ardingly Clown Academy and Crematorium in compliance with the deceased's wishes.

<<<<<<<<>>>>>>>

Classified Advertisements

Prototype Air-propelled Screep-Levelling Scrim-belt. SCDM registered
Only used once. Unwanted gift

Genuine Arthur Maudsleydale Sanitary Gun lubricating spatula. No time wasters please. 12 guineas.

FOR SALE Husband. Comes with own armchair and collection of airfix model cars. No sensible offer refused.

Learn to make lovely gifts from old newspapers and eggshells. Free booklet, just send £25.00 p&p.

Hurry while stocks last. Only three quarters of an inch left. Don't delay call today.

FOUND One large boa constric....

Ideas for sale. Some really good. 50p each.

Abbot Fish Moog Poster (nude on moped) £3.00

Found in large red box by the roadside. Huge quantity of stamps, all stuck to envelopes with addresses written on them.

Lost. 1 perfectly good mind.

Whole bag of mauve. £4.50

<<<<<<<<>>>>>>>

Antiques And Collectables.

Job lot of broken Satsuma-ware. A snip at £24,000. Contact D. Barrington c/o The Editors.

Wanted
1 Large Boa Constrictor

<<<<<<<<>>>>>>>

Ye olde advertisement for you delectation
The Most Sovereign Contraption Introduced for The Comfort of Gentlemen
Arthur Maudsleydale's
Gonad Balconette

Lubricated with premium eucalyptus paste and extracts of foreign exotica, designed by the esteemed Arthur Maudsleydale for the purpose of providing dignified regional support for noblemen of considerable proportions. Only seven Pounds, fyve Shillings and Tuppence. The lubricated balconette's superior design and tensioned cat-gut webbing grasp the Nethers for added Vigour and enhancement for today's wearers of fashionable restrictive breeches.

(Note: There have been reports of slight discomfiture when walking long distances. There will be no refunds, you are advised by the manufacturer to stop walking long distances.)

<<<<<<<<<>>>>>>>>

From the Help The Stupid Egomaniacs Dept.

STET CHETSON CROONS 20 COUNTRY AND WESTERN CLASSICS

THE INIMITABLE AND OFTEN EXCRUCIATING VOCAL YOWLINGS OF STET CHETSON BROUGHT TO YOU IN ONE GLORIOUS, OVERPRICED CD PACKAGE.

HITS INCLUDE: (Hits!! Hahahahaha!)

* ME AND THAT OLE PIG O'MINE
* THEM DARN HORNS DUN GOT ME GOING AGAIN
* TEARS ON MY LASSO
* MY COUSIN ELWOODIE
* YOU PICKED A FINE TIME TO TELL ME PAPA WAS A DANCING BOY
* CATTLE PROD AT MIDNIGHT
* YOU WHOOPED MY ASS SO BAD MA MALONEY
* YEEHAW I'M A COMIN'
* THAT AIN'T NO SADDLE BAG THAT'S MY WOMAN
* THE HOME COOKED WHORES OF STET
* ME AND THAT OLE PIG O'MINE (REGGAE VERSION)
* PEGGY-LOO'S GINGHAM SMOCK
* BAREBACK BILLYBOB
* ME AND THAT OLE PIG O'MINE (HIP HOP)
* ROOTIN' AN' A TOOTIN' UP A RED RAM'S RUMP

<<<<<<<<<>>>>>>>>

The Egerton Review

Things you never wanted to know, told to you by people who know nothing about them

Vol. 1　　　　　　　　　　　　　　　　　　　　　　　March 2004

Our Ex-Chairman Stet (Porky) Chetson. Self-made pink oboe expert and prat.

NEW CHAIRMAN LEAVES THE REVIEW

Following a bit of a disagreement, Stet Chetson is no longer our Chairman. He still hasn't sold his ranch; He never calls and quite frankly he's become something of an embarrassment.

We suspect Stet is delusional, he has, after all been telling the tabloids that none of our columnists exist! Stet bases his deductions on the fact that he hasn't actually met any of the columnists despite requesting to do so during a photo session orchestrated by us during which Stet was asked to dress up in a few different hats. What a complete lunatic. By the way, if you play Stet's C&W album backwards the words 'I'm a total fraud" can be clearly heard.

Well, March, who would have guessed that this pathetic magazine would still be going. In this issue's Editorial we bring you news of our columnists. The Beauderriere v de Verucca case continues, no murders yet but here's hoping eh? And the rumours about Neville Slipton's facial surgery are absolute rubbish. Well, just look at him.

Darcy Copperfield was recently invited to an Arse of the Week presentation and clad in his most revealing breeches; he attended in the hope of winning the title. He won but only later discovered that the bronze Bum On A Rope trophy he so proudly displayed on his mantelpiece was in fact the booby prize.

He was voted Arse*hole* of The Week, so the trousers were a waste of time. Marjorie Kyte-Hopper went toad-sexing in the Cotswolds much to the delight of local people (and very possibly the toads) who relentlessly took the piss out of her.

Rick Faberge opened a nightclub recently. Unfortunately, he used a jemmy and a house brick. The owner took him to court and Rick was cautioned for breaking and entering. Aren't people over the top?

Rick has inadvertently given the club more publicity than they could ever have dreamed of. Kev Mugton's Fuzzy Felts Exhibition attracted fewer visitors than expected. A three year old who did visit said he found the exhibits naive but noted that many of the pieces showed a preschool dexterity level.

Oh, and Dorset Barrington is in prison. Madness isn't it?

<<<<<<<<>>>>>>>

Funny Bits
Doctor: "I am very sorry to say that I have two rather bits of bad news for you".
Patient: "Oh dear, what is it?"
Doctor: "I'm afraid you have only 24 hours to live?
Patient: Oh dear, but what other thing could be as bad as that?
Doctor: I tried all day yesterday to contact you....

<<<<<<<<>>>>>>>

Darcy Copperfield's
Literature Unleashed

At the tender age of ten Darcy Copperfield was expelled from St. Peregrine's School for Boys for writing 'Anne of Green Gables is a nymphomaniac' on the blackboard. How times have changed, nowadays Copperfield's observations about sex and perversion in literature are respected and salivated over worldwide.

Shakespeare What Was In His Pounce Pot?

What is it with Shakespeare, most of his works are a load of old rubbish and should be updated for the modern world:

Much Ado About Nothing should read; Much Ado About Sod All.: Three and a half hours of theatrical bollocks put on solely for the season ticket holders to enjoy.

King Lear should read; King Lech: Old King is bothered by his three daughters attitude to his erotic drawing collection.

The Merchant of Venice should read; The Merchant-Ivory of Venice: Two period costume drama makers visit the city of canals to get a piece of the action.

Romeo and Juliet should read; Alfa-Romero and Juliet: 13yr old nymphomaniac falls in love with an Italian car

Julius Caesar should read; Julius Seizure: Roman General falls victim to a heart attack thereby foiling attempts to assassinate him. Well, if he hadn't existed, we would have had to invent him, wouldn't we....Shakespeare I mean!

COULD YOU WRITE EROTIC FICTION?

Send your exotic fantasies, in the form of a short story, to Darcy Copperfield c/o The Egerton Review for use in any other edition of the Review or for Darcy's personal files. Please include a photograph of yourself. Sorry we can't return submissions.

<<<<<<<<<>>>>>>>

...The End

The end of a clichéd story for those who can't be bothered to read a whole book.

We have all looked at and picked up a book thinking that's interesting, thumbed through it and then put it down and perhaps later wished you had read it. Here is a book you may have done that to précised here for your convenience.

A Cardigan Each
By Rosalind Pilchard

Story so far: Norma, a floral clad woman of retirement age has moved to a quaint village to pursue a peaceful lifestyle. When she has lived in the village for over six years, she becomes part of the furniture and, despite the inconvenience caused by the locals constantly mistaking her for a wing-back armchair, falls in love with Rodney.

Rodney is a professional suede elbow patch restorer and part time twitcher (person of ornithological bent) who has lived with his mother all his life. When he first meets Norma he is taken aback by her unconventionality; she wears open-toe sandals and has been abroad twice.

Despite the social and mental chasm that divides them, Rodney and Norma embark upon a completely boring relationship and intend to announce their engagement in the local paper....now read on*!*

"Only another four weeks Rodney, and we shall be man and wife" piped Norm She looked across the restaurant table at her soon-to-be-husband. Norma was happy and was eager to do all the little things that wives do for their husbands. "I hope everything is ready for the big day,

Norma," said Rodney in his nasally twang that first drew Norma to his side. Norma nodded, "Mmm," said Norma her mouth full of broccoli.

She swallowed hard. "Everything's arranged, church, vicar, cars, I don't think we've missed anything." Rodney and Norma walked through the village hand in hand.

"We're very lucky to live in this wonderful place, aren't we darling?" said Norm Rodney squeezed her hand. "Yes, beloved, there's so much of nature around us, the flora and the fauna And we've got such a lovely cottage to live in, nice garden, what more can we want."

They walked to the little stone bridge over the river and looked at the water.

"I'll tell you what I haven't seen much of lately," said Rodney. "What's that my love!" purred Norm

"Tits, Great Tits, Little Tits. I've seen plenty of woodcocks, thrushes, and lots of other birds, but I'd really like to get to grips with a pair of tits. Norma fingered her blouse buttons for a moment but though better of it.

As they walked on Rodney stopped suddenly.

"Oh No! There is something I've forgotten, the bridesmaids, I haven't got anything for the bridesmaids.

They both thought for a moment, then Norma looked up and smiled at Rodney.

"Don't worry, I know exactly what they would like, we'll get them a cardigan each." Rodney smiled, "Lovely idea" ...**The End.**

<<<<<<<<>>>>>>>

Funny Bits
I remember all my mistakes, after all, I was there for most of them!

<<<<<<<<>>>>>>>

Neville Slipton's
Language Workshop
My tongue is my passport

Neville Slipton was born Susan Grace Sliptonova in 1956. His deep interest in, and unrivalled grasp of, languages stemmed from living in a multi-lingual environment in no less than forty-three countries. He is never happier than when he is being able to use his talent with his tongue in any corner of the world.

Buying in a Foreign Land

Not so long ago I happened to be strolling, a touch of lightness in my step, along the narrow cobbled streets of Naples.

"Champignons!" I exclaimed to myself as my chiffon waistcoat became ensnared on the horns of a passing goat. It was then I realised, in a flash of *fleur de lis*, that chiffon is not commonly worn amongst peasants. Have they learned nothing from Gina Lollobrigida I wonder? But I digress. Dressing appropriately when abroad is a real skill, fine if you're me, the sort of person who floats on a cushion of supreme confidence all over the world.

But what about those of you, your Foreign-English dictionary clasped nervously to your chests, who simply haven't a clue?

Well, the first thing to remember is that your luggage, unless you're travelling by private jet, is likely to end up lost in Richard Branson's cargo chute or some such hell hole.

So, in order to maintain your *frere jacques* you'll need to know how to purchase stylish garments whether you're in the Gobi desert or simply back-packing in Beverley Hills. The easy to remember phrase below will set you on the right path to being clad, head to foot, in something simply gorgeous. Warning:

Try to remember that many people from other lands have never read Harpers & Queen. So, *Buona Notte Mon Petit Filou*. Until next time.

In English: "Hello sweet, reasonably priced seamstress found in a back street. Please run me up a flattering cerise cat-suit. I dress to the left."

In French: "Bonjour l'ouvrière couturière douce et raisonnablement eue le prix indiqué a trouvé dans une rue arrière. Veuillez me courir vers le haut d'un chat-costume flatteur de cerise. Je m'habille au gauche.

In German: "Hallo fand süsse, angemessen veranschlagte Näherin in einer rückseitigen Straße. Lassen Sie mich bitte herauf eine schmeichelnde cerise Katze-Klage laufen. Ich kleide nach links."

In Italian: Ciao il seamstress dolce e ragionevolmente valutato ha trovato in una via osterior. Faccialo funzionare prego su un gatto-vestito adulatorio del cerise. Mi vesto il a sinistra.

<<<<<<<<<>>>>>>>

at home with....
The Beauderrieres

Lord Beauderriere, in his ignorance, believes that the general viewing public is chomping at the bit to hear of the exploits of this dissolute excuse for an aristocrat. To our eyes, it's just a feeble ruse to relive his salad days. He prefers to use this picture of himself.

A SCRIPT FOR TELEVISION

EPISODE 3: LORD BEAUDERRIERE AND HIS BUTLER

SCENE 1 (IN WHICH LORD BEAUDERRIERE IS FIRM AND HARD)

CAST:

LORD B - AN ARISTOCRAT
LUNGE   - LORD B'S FAITHFUL BUTLER
INT: LORD BEAUDERRIERE'S WINE CELLAR

LORD B. IS SITTING, HIS BUTTOCKS STRAINING, IN A TATTERED WICKER CHAIR.

LORD BEAUDERRIERE:
I say, Stynky, what are the chances of fitting this on a silver salver?

LUNGE:
Put it away sir!

LORD BEAUDERRIERE:
I'm very rich and important you snivelling retainer.
Cop hold of this or I'll report you to the Caliph of Baghdad.

LUNGE:
I don't think that is part of my duties, my Lord

LORD BEAUDERRIERE:
Stynk, you must always read the small print!

In the next issue Lord Beauderriere and his Dog.

<<<<<<<<<>>>>>>>>

The Egerton Review is also sponsored by:
WAGSTAFF AND FROGJELLY
Purveyors of Soliloquy
Linctus's and Balms since 1756

Side Effects: May cause users to speak for a very long time on one subject. Groin Weakness, bruising. Can cause premature ejaculation, Irregular shaped legs, Diarrhoea and Thickening and Browning of the urine and the tendency to use contradictory terminology.

<<<<<<<<<>>>>>>>>

Countess de Verucca's
Liquid Lunch

The Countess has failed to provide a brief biography for our readers' benefit. Therefore, we telephoned her in order to ask a few questions.

Unfortunately, she was otherwise engaged with her old friend Guiseppe Uccello and although she promised, in a rather slurred voice, to call us back Pronto, she didn't.

The Countess lives in Monaco and regularly campaigns for the abolition of alcohol-free beverages. We apologise for the appalling transcript, but the Countess gave us her column early one morning on our rather old answering machine, we have done our best.

Social Drinking

Duis autem vel eum iriure dolor in hendrerit in vulputate velit esse consequat, vel illum dolore eu shit-faced feugiat nulla facilisis at rat-arsed vero eros et accumsan et hendrerit in vulputate velit esse molestie consequat, half a gallon of meths vel illum dolore eu feugiat null aiusto odio dig nissim.

Duis autem vel eum iriure dolor in hendrerit in vulputate velit esse consequat, vel illum dolore eu feugiat nulla facilisis at vero eros et Johnnie Walker Export accumsan et hendrerit in vulputate velit esse molestie consequat, vel illum dolore Savoy Grill eu feugiat null aiusto odio dig nissim out on my arse. Dolor sit amet, consectetuer adipiscing elit, sed diam nonummy nibh euismod my local off-licence tincidunt ut laoreet dolore magna aliquam erat half a dozen' cans of Special Brew volutpat. Ut wisi enim ad minim veniam, quis nostrud exerci tation ullamcorper suscipit lobortis nisl ut aliquip ex ea commodo consequat.

Duis autem vel eum iriure credit card cancelled! Dolor in hendrerit in vulputate velit esse consequat, vel illum dolore eu feugiat nulla facilisis at vero eros et accumsan et hendrerit in six bottles of Chateau

Rothschild vulputate velit four cases of Bollinger esse molestie consequat, vel illum dolore eu feugiat null aiusto two packets of Cheese and Onion crisps odio dig nissim.

Dolor sit amet, consectetuer adipiscing elit, sed diam nonummy nibh euismod tincidunt ut laoreet called the police dolore magna aliquam erat night in the cells volutpat. Ut wisi hidden a hip flask enim ad minim knickers veniam, quis nostrud exerci tation ullamcorper suscipit lobortis nisl ut aliquip ex ea commodo consequat.

Duis autem vel eum iriure returnee to the off-licence dolor in hendrerit in vulputate velit esse pissed in the window consequat, vel illum dolore eu feugiat nulla facilisis at vero eros et accumsan et hendrerit in vulputate velit White Lightning Cider esse molestie.

<<<<<<<<>>>>>>>

The Egerton Review is also sponsored by: Sister Bernadette Mahogarty's
Celibacy Candles

Side Effects: Hot wax can damage your thighs, do not use when ignited. Wax damaged thighs May cause users to speak for a very long time on one subject. Groin Weakness, bruising, Can cause premature ejaculation, Irregular shaped legs, Diarrhoea and Thickening and Browning of the urine and the tendency to use contradictory terminology.

<<<<<<<<>>>>>>>

'Zen' Sven's
Sphere of Enigma

Note for readers. Unlike our other columnists 'Zen' Sven declined to be photographed. He believes that a visual image of him might detract from the serious and fascinating nature of his column.

The Loch Ness Monster It's Real!
I thought that a couple of days camping at Loch Ness would be beneficial to my health and perhaps do a little investigation on the Monster. There was a tapping on my tent, so I got out and saw a man

in a kilt standing near my camp. "Good-day to you sir," said the man, and then he went on to ask me if I was up there for the 'beastie.'

I replied that I was actually on holiday. He introduced himself as Hamilton McCurdle and that he had seen the Monster over 1000 times. I offered him a cup of tea, but he refused and took a can of Special Brew out of his sporran. I asked him about the Loch Ness Monster, what did it look like

"Och, it's a strange looking beastie. Not as big as you would think, but a moonster all the same." I asked this very intelligent man; what sort of size is it. "It's aboot as big as a log, in fact, out of the 1000 sightings I expect it was a log aboot 999 times.!" I was caught up in the magic of this,

"So, the monster is some gigantic primeval log that haunts the loch?" He looked at me, at least I think he did as his eyes were obscured by the thick lenses of his spectacles. "I didna say it was gigantic, I said it was a big as a log." This made me think. As we sat there musing on this another kilted gentleman walked up.

"Good morning to you Hamilton, and to you stranger."

Mr McCurdle stood up, swayed a bit, and replied,

"Good morning to you, Hector." I said my good mornings and offered Hector a cup of tea, which he declined in favour of a can of Special Brew from Mr McCurdle's sporran.

"So, you've come to see the 'beastie'?" said Hector. I explained that I was on holiday and was interested in the Monster.

"I've seen it y'ken," said Hector. I was most fortunate to meet two locals who had intimate knowledge of the monster.

"I was coming oot the pub late one night and got inta me boot to go across to me cottage. Aboot half across, och, my knees still tremble at the thought of it, right in front of me this thing reared up in front me boot."

I was all agog, at last a first encounter sighting from some who knows the loch like the back of his hand. I asked him to go on, but he seemed to be looking at the back of his hand mystified. I asked Hector to go on.

"Gone on aboot what?" he asked. "What was it you saw in the loch."

"Ah, the beastie y'mean, ay, there is was still on the water, looking at me with its dark eye, it was magical!"

"What did it look like?" I enquired.

"Looked like, a bloody great log, that's what it looked like, not gigantic mind you, but big, I turned and rowed for the bank, I didn't what to meet it again."

The two men sauntered off fortified by the Special Brew and the ten pound note I had given them each.

I came away from Loch Ness confident in the knowledge that I had met two remarkable men, who in their wisdom tried to deflect my enquiries, but only convinced me that there was something unknown in the deep waters of Loch Ness, not gigantic, but unknown.

<<<<<<<<>>>>>>>

Witty Man
He's got an answer for everything!
"So, I said to them, sack me at your peril!"

Sorry, Witty Man seems to be feeling a bit defensive. Obviously, he doesn't want to lose his job so he's on probation. We've told him, say something funny next month or you're out!

<<<<<<<<>>>>>>>

Dr Makitupp Azugoalong's
Quick Clinic

All too aware that medical jargon and detailed diagnoses can worry patients, Dr Azugoalong, an Iron Maiden fan, set up the first on-line Monosyllabic Medical Response Clinic in 1998.. Dr Azugoalong speaks very little English.

Dear Doctor Azugoalong,
Is it possible to catch a mental illness from a magazine? I've been reading The Egerton Review and thoroughly enjoying it, yet my friends and family all say I am mad. Are they right?
Yes.

Dear Doctor Azugoalong,
Have you ever had the funny feeling that you're being watched?
Yes.

Dear Doctor Azugoalong,
When you've had that feeling that you're being watched do you think it is because you actually are, or do you think it is because you are suffering from paranoia? I think you are probably paranoid...are you?
Yes.

Dear Doctor Azugoalong,
I've been watching you.
Oh.

Dear Doctor Azugoalong,
Still think you're paranoid.
No.

Dear Doctor Azugoalong,
Would you please send back my x-rays? The lounge looks so bare without them. Can I expect them by return post?
No.

Dear Doctor Azugoalong,
Are you really mono-syllabic or do you sometimes speak normally using multi-syllable words?
Yes and No.

Please note that Dr. Azugoalong is not a Gynaecologist no matter how hard he insists he is!

<<<<<<<<>>>>>>>

An Advertisement from the editors of The Egerton Review

Would you like to earn a fortune enjoying yourself and writing silly thing all day long? Well wouldn't we all?
What makes you you're so different? Maybe it's time to get real and come to terms with the fact that no-one gets rich by being silly. Except us, eventually, at least that's the plan.

Public Eye
your observations appreciated
doppelgangers

We invite you to send in examples of look-alikes. Only the most astounding resemblances will be published

DJ Draycott observes.

My next door neighbour looks exactly like the man who lives opposite me. They deny being twins which makes the similarity between them all the more astounding. What do the readers think?

Children say the funniest things

Janet Monks shares this with us: *"My daughter Bethany didn't want to go to bed one night.*

When I told her that she must go to bed to get her beauty sleep she said," " No mummmmeeee leave me alone you bitch I hate you. I want a drink of water aggggghh don't smack me mummy please I'll phone Childline if you ever leave burn marks again..."

How we laughed!

you'll never guess who I saw...

Charlotte Dunkley spotted: Cruella De Ville at Crufts. "I was astonished to see her there as I thought she was banned.

Beauderriere/de Verucca Kerfuffle

Lord Beauderriere, on whom our script for television is based, announced that he has written, and intends to publish, a biography of the Countess de Verucca, our very own in-house wines and spirits connoisseur.

Beauderriere's book, an unauthorised account of the Countess's life, has caused uproar amongst the upper echelons of Italian society. The Countess herself permitted a reproduction of the letter she sent to Beauderriere; here we have a letter in support of his Lordship.

La Santiado Police Force
The Guardhouse Government Square
Santiado Island of Calamari

Dear Meester Hanns,
Hullo, itsa me, Migual Bastado, Police Chief, big man in Calamari no. You willa probly heerd by now of the fantastico new book that isa bin writ by my good fren da Count de Beauderriere , grate personal fren, he comma ere alla tarm.

I fink itsa bout time that summerone put up the finger an probed da Countess as she assa bin nuffin but a pain ina my hears for a long tarm cummin now. She causes da trubble alla der tarm, wiv'r drinkin an afondlin of my officers whena dey incastrate her.

She try alla tarm to pretend to be aal sweeteners and lightenin, but no, she bloody cow she is, and I have told her that she is person au gratin on this island and good riding to her. The Count is rite in ever fing he say abart her. The Count is a hombre who is always upright and rigid like all British knobs and I willa have nuffink sed abart im.
Miguel Bastado

<<<<<<<<<>>>>>>>>

Funny Bits
Moses descended from Mount Sinai and looks at the waiting Israelites.
Moses: "I have good news and bad news."

Israelites: "What's the good news"

Moses: I've got them down to ten"

Israelites: "What's the bad news"

Moses: "Adultery is still in!"

<<<<<<<<<>>>>>>>>

Rick Faberge's Column
"Even some thing's I don't like are expensive"

Rick is indisposed after a rather hectic week at the races, hopefully he'll be back next month! He did send some content in, but it was

written on the back of a betting slip in pencil! Couldn't read it sorry. It was probably puerile drivel anyway!

<<<<<<<<>>>>>>>

Kev Mugton's
Fine Art Course

Kev Mugton shot to fame after a brief appearance on TV when he famously miscut some MDF and emulsioned a 17th century marble fireplace. Kev has always been interested in painting but has no experience whatsoever. Kev also hopes to win the Mastermind Rose Bowl too but that's unlikely as he is fundamentally thick as two miscut planks.

Masterpieces Compared

Wotcha, I think that what I do is Art. It's no different to Leonardo De Caprio painting his Moaning Lisa to me putting emulsion on a wall. Anyway, this month I have decided to compare The Vauxhall Cavalier by Frank Halls to The Scream by Edward Munchkin.

I mean what's the Cavalier got to laugh about. I mean he lost the Civil War, and his boss got his head cut off. And that idiot on the bridge, if he didn't like crossing bridges, why did he cross it.

What does he do, run across, no he creeps across and then stands there holding his head and reacting to a scream. Get a bleeding life. Mind you, lucky Munchkin was there with his paints, eh?

<<<<<<<<>>>>>>>

Hollywood Interviews

Each month one of our Columnists interview a famous Hollywood Star. This month Darcy Copperfield talks to Fifi LaRoche. Her films credits include Lust: Twenty Times A Night, and I'm A Nun, Help

Me Get Out Of This Habit! Ms. LaRoche now runs her own Casting Agency.

Darcy: Well, Fifi, it's a pleasure to meet you at last. I have all the films you made. Mmm, could you tell our readers how you started in the business?

Fifi: You mean in the movie business? Well, it all started when I was working as a waitress in a cocktail bar....No, No, wait a minute, that's not right, that's a song isn't it. Oh, I remember, I was a hooker in Las Vegas and one of my clients turned out to be a movie producer and the rest is history.

Darcy: So, So, umm, this, movie director got you signed to one of the big studios?

Fifi: Not exactly... are you all right? You seem to be sweating a bit, anyway, he said my talent wasn't in actually acting, he said I had something more than that, something deeper.
He signed me to Erotic Studios, and I started making films straightaway. Sometimes as many as five or six a day!

Darcy: Was it, was it, umm, rather strange, y'know, naked and doing it, doing it with all those camera people watching? Watching as your slim, lithe body twisted into all sorts of positions, glistening, swelling, opening like an oyst.... I, I....

It was after this that the interview was terminated due to Darcy being knocked unconscious by one of Fifi's stiletto heels.

<<<<<<<<<>>>>>>>>

Marjorie Kyte-Hopper's
Guide to Life

'Auntie' Marjorie Kyte-Hopper's career as Advisor to the World began when, as a Brownie, she started bossing people about and giving her opinions freely.' She lives in Norfolk with her dog Attila Marjorie, much to her astonishment, is a gay icon.

Rubber For All

Last week I read in my local paper that our vicar is a rubber fetishist. Needless to say, there are some members of the parish who are shocked by the news. Aren't we English a stuffy lot? It's alright for us to be fetishists but not the vicar. I was so outraged by some people's narrow views that I staged a revolt on the village green.

I myself am a rubber fetishist. I think it's simply marvellous stuff, I get through, on average, nearly two pairs of marigolds per day, more if I'm gardening or going to have anything to do with the boy scouts.

And as for always having a rubber on the end of my HB, well I'm never without one.

It's so easy, when jotting down a recipe for a friend, to make a mistake. Swiftly on to Wellingtons then. Here in the countryside a decent pair of hard-wearing Wellingtons is a must.

I favour the green Stanley Eversfield boot with fleecy lining, they are a little more expensive but so durable and impervious to most wet substances that extra expense is well spent.

A rubber sheet when picnicking always comes in handy. Eleanor Lavishe (A Room With A View) never went anywhere without her Mackintosh Squares. I suppose that makes her a rubber fetishist too. Poo bah to this silly tendency to sneer at users of rubber. When will we realise that we are all users? The tyres on your motor vehicle are made from rubber but you wouldn't expect to be banned from buying a ticket to the Gang Show because of it would you? I always say it takes all kinds of people to make the bright and beautiful world we live in. *Auntie Marjorie*

<<<<<<<<<>>>>>>>>

The Cloud Cuckoo Report
Thoughts on Strange and Obscure Complaints

NUT FREE NUT TREES
The recent spate of gardening programmes will have inspired many of us to make improvements to our outside space. Tempting though it is, try to avoid exotic plants which generally don't fare well in our climate.

A case in hand is that of the little nut tree. These diminutive legume producing shrubs rarely give rise to a glut of nuts. More common is the appearance of a silver nutmeg and a golden pear. Garden centres are not obliged to refund your money. Moreover, owners of trees of this type are subjected to visits (often unannounced) from the King of Spain's daughter.

HOT CROSS BUNS PRICE FIXING SCANDAL
Christians are being tricked and left confused about the recommended retail price of their favourite symbolic Easter treat. Hot Cross Buns are commonly advertised as being one a penny, two a penny.

This can't be right. If you can buy two for a penny then one should be only cost a ha'penny. A pie man, who we interviewed on the way to a fayre, said,

"My pies are a penny each which represents better value than one or even two Hot Cross Buns."

To find out if the pie man's claims are true we sent intrepid reporter Nigel (who is a bit thick) to purchase one.

Unfortunately, Nigel, on account of being thick, was unable to produce the necessary funds when required to do so.

THE WATER BOARD, THE ARMY AND THE NHS MAKE MAN'S LIFE A MISERY
A man and his wife, Jill, intend to take the Water Board, The Army and the NHS to court following what he sees as atrocious behaviour from all three. The man and his wife, Jill, are required to make daily

trips to a well for their water. The well is inconveniently placed at the top of hill on which army manoeuvres frequently take place. Says, Jack, husband of Jill,

"*There is usually a ten thousand strong army going up and down the hill. This is, of course, dangerous and inconvenient. We find that most times when they are up the hill, they are up, and when they are down the hill, they are, of course, down.*

The most infuriating times occur when they are only halfway up, because then they are neither up nor down, It was during one of these hiatuses that an accident occurred to both me and my wife, Jill."

"*We had just gone up the hill to get a pail of water when I fell down and broke my crown, my wife, Jill, came tumbling after. I complained to the officer in charge, a rather grand old man of noble bearing, but could not receive any understanding.*

Both myself and my wife, Jill, made our way to the local hospital and after waiting for over four hours we were fobbed off with a concoction of vinegar and brown paper to mend our heads. We have received no apology from the water board, army officer or the hospital. We are out of water and are dreading our trip to the well tomorrow."

MAN, RELENTLESSLY PURSUED BY BELLS

Waking to the sound of church bells may not be as relaxing and peaceful as it seems. A frustrated reader comments.

"*I moved to London recently and bought a comfortable apartment near St Clements Church. I was woken abruptly one Sunday morning by the bells which were constantly ringing on about two kinds of citrus fruit.*

I tolerated this for a few weeks but eventually the strain got to me, and I had to move house. I settled near St Martins Church when one Sunday morning I was woken abruptly by the bells informing me that I owe them three farthings.

This is absurd as I have never owed anybody money at any time, especially not money that is no longer legal tender. I tolerated this for a few weeks but felt, once more, that I had to move on. I found a pleasant bijou residence near the Old Bailey.

I was woken abruptly one Sunday morning by the bells asking me to give a payment date for the three farthings that I assure I do not owe.

I moved to a bungalow in Shoreditch only to be woken abruptly one Sunday morning by the bells informing that they will pay the

outstanding amount of three farthings when they are in funds. I can no longer leave the house. Is this campanology gone mad?"

CORNISH NASTY
A bigamist, reported to have no less than seven wives, accosted a walker who was on route to St Ives. The bigamist's wives had produced several sons each causing the walker to attempt to solve a trick mathematical problem. *"It was really weird, but I have no witnesses to the incident as I was the only one going to St Ives.*

<<<<<<<<>>>>>>>
Dorset Barrington's
Antique ~~Dealing~~ Stealing

THIS PAGE HAS BEEN CANCELLED AS THE COLUMNIST IN PRISON FOR THEFT OF ANTIQUES. HE DENIES THE CHARGES SAYING HE WAS JUST LOOKING AFTER IT FOR SOMEONE. AS DORSET IS A COMPULSIVE LIAR AND THIEF, HE WAS NOT BELIEVED AND IS NOW RESIDING AT HMP GRYMTHORPE

<<<<<<<<>>>>>>>

The Egerton Review is also sponsored by:
HOBSON GRONK'S DANDRUFF AGITATOR
*Not recommended for use by those with dormant dandruff

Side Effects: Severe headaches, agitation and dandruff, . Wax damaged thighs   May cause users to speak for a very long time on one subject. Groin Weakness, bruising, Can cause Irregular shaped legs, Diarrhoea and Thickening and Browning of the urine and the tendency to use contradictory terminology.

<<<<<<<<>>>>>>>

In the Potting Shed with Old Nobby
A Selection of Non-Motivational Quotes from our resident miserable old git!

"There are only two things you need to know to become rich and powerful; Don't tell ANYONE everything you know! And ....!"

<<<<<<<<>>>>>>>

HUMOUR FROM THE 19th CENTURY
Son: "What makes the world go round Father?"
Father: "Usually about 4 whiskies my son!"

<<<<<<<<>>>>>>>

It has just occurred to me that we have never seen Old Nobby used the staff toilets. He carries a brown paper carrier bag tied tightly at the top with string. I have informed Security never, NEVER ask to see what's in the bag!

<<<<<<<<>>>>>>>

Millicent 1940's Wife
War is nearly over and people throughout England are looking forward to a bright new future

You haven't been having ideas again have you poppet?

Only silly ones that would probably make us rich Dwarling.

Dwarling?" said Millicent smoothing her floral apron happily.

"Would you be awfully cross if I invented an innovative television programme?" Millicent's husband Gordon put his copy of Manly Things Weekly down and looked at his wife querulously.

"Now Millsy," he said with a care-worn smile, "you simply must get these silly ideas out of your head. You invent something every month and quite frankly I find it unbecoming. And anyway, there's the White Elephant stall to think about and weren't you supposed to be resetting old Mrs Hartlepool's victory roll this afternoon?"

"Yes, I know Dwarling." said Millicent quickly making an exquisite ball gown out of some scraps of newspaper. "I wasn't think of inventing the television programme now!" she laughed, "I plan to wait until the late 1990's, after all, Susan and Robert will be dead by then, so I'll have more time."

Gordon sighed and, polishing his Bakelite brogues, said, "Come on you old ninny, let's not have any more talk about inventions.

You've got to think about broiling that old sow for supper and didn't I overhear you offering to help demolish the Jones's Anderson Shelter?"

Millicent bowed her head, "Yes Dwarling," she said mournfully, "but I just thought that inventing a really popular television programme would get us out of this dreadful, dreadful financial mess.

I've thought it all through, the contestants on the show would be normal people who crave fame and fortune, the camera's would be on them constantly and I thought I'd call it 'Large Sibling.' Gordon adjusted his Bakelite tiepin and stood up. He grasped the tea trolley, upsetting Millicent's freshly made Parsnip Knickerbocker Glory.

He was angry now. "We went through all this when you had the lame idea of inventing a machine that washed, spun and dried our clothes. Now let's just forget all about your pie in the sky ideas, you sit and listen to the BBC Home Service, and I'll get us both a glass of cordial, shall I?" Millicent smiled to herself. Gordon was a completely wonderful husband, "Promise you're not awfully cross Dwarling." she pleaded.

<<<<<<<<<>>>>>>>>

Foreign Phrases for Everyday Use
Compiled by Neville Slipton

Just a few helpful hints for those trips abroad hope you find them useful, bye, love you X

In English: *One loaf of bread and 40 kilos of bringle-shoot biscuits please kind baker with cheeks of rosy-hue.*

In German: Ein Laib Brot und 40 kilos von bringle-schießen Hanfbisluite gefallen freundlichem Bäcker mit Backen der Rosigfarbe.

In Italian: Una pagnotta di pane e 40 chili de bringle-sparano i biscotti della canapa soddisfano il panettiere gentile con le guancie della ottimistico-tonalità.

In Spanish: Un pan de pan y 40 kilos de bringle-tiran a las galletas del cáñamo satisfacen a panadero bueno con las mejillas de la atractivo-tonalidad.

(Please note that there is not a French translation for the above due to the on-going Anglo-French Bringle-Shoot War. We mention this because we don't want you thinking we couldn't be arsed to do a French translation. Ed.)

In English: *Please could you direct me to the Arthur Maudsleydale Museum of Torture which I believe to be situated somewhere near the Poppleton Cathedral in the market square. Thank you, kind plump peasant woman, with cheeks of rosy-hue and characterful wizened visage.*

In German: *Konnten bitte Sie direkt ich zum Arthur Maudsleydale Museum der Folterung, dem ich glaube, nahe der Poppleton Kathedrale in Marktquadrat irgendwo aufgestellt zu werden. Danke freundliche pralle ländliche Frau mit Backen der rosigen Farbe und charaktervolles Gesicht*

In Italian: *Potreste prego diretti meal museo del Arthur Maudsleydale do tortura che credo per essere situato in qualche luogo vicino alla cattedrale di Poppleton nel quadrato del mercato. Grazie donna agricola grassoccia gentile con le guancie della tonalità ottimistica e charactterful wizened il visage.*

<<<<<<<<>>>>>>>

HUMOUR FROM THE 19ᵗʰ CENTURY
"What is the difference between a tube and a foolish Dutchman? One is a hollow cylinder and the other a silly Hollander."

<<<<<<<<>>>>>>>

Letters from our Readers
The following is a selection of the boring dreary rubbish sent to us by readers of the magazine.

Dear Editors at The Egerton Review,
Last month an unhinged and deluded inmate from the Fookes Mogton-Crank Psychiatric Centre in Birmingham wrote to your letters page. Dan Graves (not his real name) claimed to have lost touch with his feminine side. This is a lie. He has not lost touch with his feminine side and was last seen heading towards your offices wearing a Laura Ashley pinafore dress and sling-backs. Please do approach this man. He is a nutcase (official).
Dr Romeo Lettuce.
Please could you be more specific with regard to details. The above description (pinafore dress and sling-backs) could apply to many members of our Editorial staff. Therefore, it would be virtually impossible for us to identify your unhinged and deluded escapee were he to mingle here in our offices. We are very frightened. The Editors

Dear Editors at The Egerton Review,
Why are you never in your office? I have tried on many occasions to speak to one of you but you're never there. I'm beginning to wonder if you actually exist.
'Zen' Sven
P.S I'm Swedish, does that matter?
If you were truly psychic 'Zen,' you'd know when we are due to be in our office. The Editors P.S. We do exist. Spooky isn't it?

Dear Editors at The Egerton Review,
It did not escape my notice that your publication appears to include a lot of boa constrictor references. Is this because you are, like me, fascinated by these marvellous creatures or is it just that you find the things inexplicably funny and are unable to drop the subject even though others might not get the joke?
Mr. Hector Slithe.
We are not, by any means, obsessed with boa constrictors. We merely report the facts. We do, however, have an in-house boa constrictor who is very tame. The Ed..... arggghhh Only joking

Dear Editors at The Egerton Review,
Where can I buy a book of funny sayings? I'm desperate.
Witty Man.
Sorry, it would be pointless us providing you with a source of witticisms. If we went that far we might as well write your column for you. The Editors

Dear Editors at The Egerton Review,
Is your publication available in Sweden?
Jan Engelsson
P.S I live in Sweden, does that matter?
Our magazine is available worldwide Jan. We can't see that it matters if you live in Sweden. It's your choice. The Editors.

<<<<<<<<>>>>>>

Classified Advertisements

SIX UNWANTED THINGS will sell separately or as a collection. Please call daytimes or evenings.

GENUINE ARTHUR MAUDSLEYDALE CLITORAL klaxon. Hardly used; Need wipe round with surgical spirit. Otherwise, immaculate. £450.00. It was good for us.

FOR SALE How to Train a Boa Constrictor (Book & CD). Only £15.00. Not really that bloodstained.

FREE TOILET ROLL TUBES available to collector. Pop in anytime.

GUN-METAL EFFECT GENTLEMAN'S HANDBAG. Never used at night. Newly-adjusted. 25 guineas.

SMALL MAN slight wear to the flanges, otherwise vgc £100 or not.

CHILDREN x 4 Owner suddenly gone off them. 40p

SIGNED UNUSED, UNWANTED copy of BIG RANCHMAN SINGS COUNTRY by Stet Chetson. £15.00

STUFF with lumps in. Hurry before they dissolve.

STOLEN

Satsuma-Ware in perfect condition but believed to have been dropped by the burglar during his getaway.

ANTIQUES & COLLECTABLES

Job lot of broken Satsuma-Ware. A snip at £23,000. Contact Dorset Barrington c/o The Editors.

PERSONAL

LOVELY OLD MAN wltm anyone who may remember him from the old days as he doesn't know where he lives.

OBITUARIES

We do not have entries for this section this month. Due to the fine weather and the new ring road, there have been no cases of death by hypothermia or accident.

Let us try and improve things for next month. We will give two £1 WH Smith Gift Vouchers for the most interesting death.

<<<<<<<<<>>>>>>>>

The Egerton Review

Things you never wanted to know, told to you by people who know nothing about them

Vol. 1   April 2004

Stet Chetson, our ex-chairman who still hasn't sold the ranch and probably deserved the spanking he got.

EX- CHAIRMAN GETS A GOOD SPANKING

Stet Chetson, looking better than he has done in a long while, is still under the illusion that he is our Chairman. He still hasn't sold his ranch. But then if you haven't got a bloody ranch, you can't sell it, can you Stet? We were seriously considering having him 'done over.' But as you can see, Somebody's done it for us.

It's April and in this issue's editorial we bring you news of our columnists. The Beauderriere v de Verucca case still continues, why anyone should be interested in a fat aristocrat and an inebriated old bag I don't know. And the rumours about Neville Slipton's facial surgery still abound but are absolute rubbish. He's always looked like that without make-up. I think the most exciting piece of news is that out fat git arsehole of an Ex-Chairman was mysteriously beaten up. There were no witnesses to the attack, but one old lady says she saw a collection of people driving away in a white van. She described then as a foppish man with long hair, a rather camp man in a yachting cap, a man in sunglasses, a Dr, a man in a white robe shouting that "all of this anger was ruining his karma," a matronly lady in heavy brogues, and a rather inebriated foreign looking woman being thrown into the back of the van by a builder.

This is of course no use as evidence because of the very poor descriptions. We wish Stet a very speedy recovery. Oh, and Dorset Barrington is still in prison. Madness isn't it? The Editors

<<<<<<<<>>>>>>>
Darcy Copperfield's
Literature Unleashed

At the tender age of ten Darcy Copperfield was expelled from St. Peregrine's School for Boys for writing 'Anne of Green Gables is a nymphomaniac' on the blackboard. How times have changed, nowadays Copperfield's observations about sex and perversion in literature are respected and salivated over worldwide.

Charles Dickens - Real life? Ha!

Well, Dickens eh, Charles Bloody Dickens. What did he really know about the poor, show me a poor person who sings and dances around after a bowl of gruel. 'Consider yerself at 'ome'? piss off more than likely.

The poor of Victorian London were after one thing and one thing alone—GIN. Little Dorritt would prostitute herself for a pennyworth of the old Geneva and I don't think it was more gruel that little Oliver wanted more of. They were all at it in Victorian London:

The Olde Curiosity Shoppe: the Olde Ginne Shoppe probably.

The Mystery of Edwin Drood: Ha, Edwin's Droop I should think, or more likely Brewer's Droop.

And now we have The Pickwick Papers: A collection of 'gentlemen' form a club. Drinking club probably. Popping off every now and then to Dingley Dell and upsetting Kathleen Harrison. Then promising to marry Mrs. Bordello and then wheedling out of it. Then there's that Sam Weller, he's so pissed he can't say his V's. They are all on the piss. Charles Dickens? it's all humbug!

COULD YOU WRITE EROTIC FICTION?
Send your exotic fantasies, in the form of a short story, to Darcy Copperfield c/o The Egerton Review for use in any other edition of the Review or for Darcy's personal files. Please include a photograph of yourself. Sorry we can't return submissions.

<<<<<<<<>>>>>>>

HUMOUR FROM THE 19th CENTURY
"See here, waiter, I've found a button in my salad."
"That's all right, sir, it's part of the dressing."

<<<<<<<<>>>>>>>

Neville Slipton's
Language Workshop
"My tongue is my passport."

Neville Slipton was born Susan Grace Sliptonova in 1956. His mother was French/Indonesian, and his father was Russian. His deep interest in, and unrivalled grasp of, languages stemmed from living in a multi-lingual environment in no less than forty-three countries.

Picture This
Last night, whilst admiring my new friend Giuseppe's gondola, I realised, a sudden feeling of excitement circulating in my Moules Marinière's that my passport photograph is absolute stunning, "Caribiniere!" I thought, "it's simply ghastly that all globetrotters (I am

the exception) make do with unflattering photographic depictions of themselves.

So, what can be done? Plenty, no need to get your broderie anglaise in a twist. Prior to having your passport photograph taken, I advise an intensive course of sun-shower treatment followed by electrolysis to remove any unwanted male hormones (this applies to both men and women). Then, remembering that you're going to be shot Capodimonte (head and shoulders only), select something eye catching for the neck are A fabulous piece of costume jewellery or a scarf should do the trick. I personally like to go for the chiselled perfection look, so it's cheeks in and a full pout. Viola!

You'll look completely Haute Cuisine and enjoy the added bonus of being able to slip into a customs officer slip through customs without making all those tiresome declarations. To recap ponce yourself up, pout and pull. The phrase below will come in handy for all kinds of official situations; I used it successfully when defending myself against charges of intention to commit an indecent act on sanctified ground.

This month Neville insisted on exercising his foreign tongue. We apologise in advance.

"Can you not tell from this lovely snap in my passport that I am just a happy-go-lucky free spirit whose au natural tendencies are entirely innocent"

In French: "*Pourvez vous ne pas dire de cette belle rupture dans mon passeport que je suis juste un heureux vais l'esprit libre chanceux dont les tendances normales d'Au sont entièrement innocentes.*"

In German: "*Können Sie nicht von diesem reizenden Schnäpper in meinem Paß erklären, daß ich ein glückliches gehe glücklicher freier Geist gerecht bun dessen natürliche Tendenzen' des Au völlig unschudig sind*"

In Italian: "*Potete non dire a da questo schiocco bello nel mio passaporto che sia giusto un felice vada spirito libero fortunato di cui tendenze naturali dell' au sono intermente non colpevoli.*"

<<<<<<<<>>>>>>>

at home with...
The Beauderriere's

Lord Beauderriere, in his ignorance, believes that the general viewing public is chomping at the bit to hear of the exploits of this dissolute excuse for an aristocrat. To our eyes, it's just a feeble ruse to relive his salad days.

A SCRIPT FOR TELEVISION

EPISODE 4: LORD BEAUDERRIERE AND HIS DOG
SCENE 1 (IN WHICH LORD BEAUDERRIERE IS FIRM)

CAST:
LORD B - A FAT ARISTOCRAT
POOPSY - LORD B'S FAITHFUL POODLE

INT: LORD BEAUDERRIERE'S DRAWING ROOM
LORD B. IS SITTING, HIS BUTTOCKS STRAINING, IN A TATTERED WICKER CHAIR.

LORD BEAUDERRIERE:
I say, Poopsy, what are the chances of you sitting on my lap?

POOPSY:
Woof, Woof!

LORD BEAUDERRIERE:
I'm very rich and important you snivelling mutt.
Come here or I'll report you to the Battersea Dogs Home.

POOPSEY
Woof, Woof

LORD BEAUDERRIERE:
I think I prefer the cat anyway.

Countess de Verucca's
Liquid Lunch

The Countess lives in Monaco and regularly campaigns for the abolition of alcohol-free beverages. We apologise for the appalling transcript, but his Countess gave us her column early one morning on our rather old answering machine, we have done our best.

Top Tipples To Tantalize

Duis autem vel eum iriure dolor in hendrerit in vulputate velit esse consequat, vel illum dolore eu shit-faced feugiat nulla facilisis at high as a kite vero eros et accumsan et hendrerit in vulputate velit esse molestie consequat, a gallon of Cointreau vel illum dolore eu feugiat null aiusto odio dig nissim.

Duis autem vel eum iriure dolor in hendrerit in vulputate velit esse consequat, vel illum dolore eu feugiat nulla facilisis at vero eros et barman looked at me funny accumsan et hendrerit in vulputate stiletto heel velit esse molestie knackers consequat, vel illum pompous wanker of a maitre de dolore. Ritz eu feugiat null not quite our sort of clientele aiusto odio dig nissim picked up bodily and forcibly ejected.

Dolor sit amet, consectetuer adipiscing elit, sed diam nonummy nibh euismod my local bar tincidunt ut laoreet dolore magna aliquam erat half a dozen' cans of Stella volutpat. Ut wisi enim ad minim veniam, quis nostrud exercitation ullam corper suscipit lobortis nisl ut aliquip ex ea commodo consequat.

Duis autem vel eum iriure would not take Euros! dolor in hendrerit in vulputate velit esse consequat, vel illum dolore eu feugiat nulla facilisis at vero eros et accumsan et hendrerit nicking six bottles of Chateau Briand vulputate velit four cases of Dubonnet esse molestie consequat, vel illum dolore eu feugiat null aiusto two packets of Cheese and Onion crisps odio dig brassiere nissim.

Dolor sit amet, consectetuer adipiscing elit, sed diam nonummy nibh euismod. Got my credit card bill tincidunt ut laoreet dolore magna aliquam erat volutpat. Have to sell the Porsche. Ut wisi enim ad minim veniam, take the pissing bus quis nostrud exercitation travel with ordinary people ullam corper suscipit lobortis nisl ut aliquip ex ea commodo consequat.

Sooner stay sober. Duis autem vel eum iriure Wine Club on the Internet dolor in hendrerit in vulputate velit esse consequat no need to leave my bed, vel illum dolore eu feugiat bonk all day with Guiseppe nulla facilisis at vero eros et accumsan et hendrerit in vulputate velit esse molestie dry throat!

<<<<<<<<<>>>>>>>

'Zen' Sven's
Sphere of Enigma

Note for readers. Unlike our other columnists 'Zen' Sven declined to be photographed. He believes that a visual image of him might detract from the serious and fascinating nature of his column. We actually believe it is because he is so devastatingly ugly that no one would ever believe a word he says.

Ghosts

I have always been interested in the Paranormal, so I was pleased to receive a letter from Peregrine Thudde, a very intelligent and admirable man. He lives in a large house on Dartmoor.

I arrived at Thudde House around eight in the evening and was made most welcome by my host. After dinner we sat in his library and discussed, what Mr Thudde described, the hideous apparition that haunts his ancient abode. "It usually appears around midnight."

I nodded and told him that this was quite normal as it is called the 'witching hour.' The apparition he described sounded as if it had been born in the very depths of HELL!! It was about 5'6" tall and is surrounded by a grey mist. "I first saw it," continued Mr Thudde, "on the upper landing. It burst out of the bathroom, swearing, shouting, all of which was unintelligible. And in its wake was the most atrocious smell." I asked him if anyone else had seen it, but he apparently lives alone in the house with only his old father for company. I went to bed that night with some trepidation.

Mr Thudde had drawn such a graphic picture of this apparition that I was not sure I wished to see it. It was in the early hours of the morning that I heard a groaning and straining sound coming from down the hall. I got out of my bed and went slowly down the hallway.

From under the bathroom door as a flickering light and it was from there that the moans came. Suddenly the door burst open, and a ghastly figure followed by a ghastly smell rushed from the bathroom and disappeared down the corridor. I left the house straight away, scared stiff and positive about the existence of ghosts.

I was sorry not to have met Mr Thudde's father who, I understand, was illness with a strange malady that causes one to have constipation and diarrhoea all at the same time. Never mind.

<<<<<<<<>>>>>>>

Witty Man
He's got an answer for everything
Ummmmmmmmm!!
Witty Man is still embarrassed because he is not as witty as he thought, I think we will sack him or at least remove his by-line.

<<<<<<<<>>>>>>>

Dr. Makitupp Azugoalong's
Quick Clinic

All too aware that medical jargon and detailed diagnoses can worry patients, Dr. Azugoalong, an Iron Maiden fan, set up the first on-line Monosyllabic Medical Response Clinic in 1998. Dr Azugoalong speaks very little English.

Dear Doctor Azugoalong
I have noticed that you have asked for sponsorship. Surely this is totally against medical ethics and could cause you to be struck off. Are you worried about this?
Yes.

Dear Doctor Azugoalong
I am a solicitor for the Medical Council, and we do not like the idea of you receiving sponsorship for your column. We will be checking up on you on a regular basis.
Shit

Dear Doctor Azugoalong
I used your recommended Anti-Scurf Shampoo recently and I have to say that my hair will never be the same ever again. It has all fallen out. I shall, of course, be reporting you to the Medical Council and, will of course, be suing the arse off you!
Oh cock!

Dear Doctor Azugoalong
I wonder if you could pass my name onto your previous correspondent. I am a solicitor with a very good track record in suing negligent Drs.
Oh, Piss Off!

Dear Doctor Azugoalong
I am a twenty year old young woman who, despite everyone saying I have the body of a Venus and that I am stunningly beautiful, needs someone to confirm this medically. Would you be willing to examine every part of my body very closely
OH MY GOD!

Please remember that Dr. Azugoalong is Not a Cosmetic Surgeon (despite what he tells you)

<<<<<<<<>>>>>>>

HUMOUR FROM THE 19th CENTURY
Why do we call a manuscript a MS?
Because that is the state in which the editor finds it.

HUMOUR FROM THE 19th CENTURY
HE: "I am a millionaire. I've got money enough for both of us?"
SHE: "Yes, if you are moderate in your tastes."

HUMOUR FROM THE 19th CENTURY
"Marriage is an institution intended to keep women out of mischief and get men into trouble."

<<<<<<<<>>>>>>>

Public Eye
your observations appreciated

doppelgangers
We invite you to send in examples of look-alikes. Only the most astounding resemblances will be published.

DJ Draycott observes.
My son Desmond is the spitting image of a man who got me pregnant when I met him, I met in Swindon, or was it Sweden? Anyway, if any of your readers know someone from Sweden or Swindon that looks like my son, they will be amazed too.
What do the readers think?

children say the funniest things
C'mon you little bastards, say something funny!!
How we didn't laugh!

HUMOUR FROM THE 19th CENTURY
"Who is the greatest chicken-killer in Shakespeare? Macbeth, because he did murder most foul."

<<<<<<<<>>>>>>>
The Beauderriere/de Verucca Kerfuffle

Lord Beauderriere, on whom our script for television is based, announced that he has written, and intends to publish, a biography of his Countess de Verucca, our very own in-house wines and spirits connoisseur.

Beauderriere's book, an unauthorised account of his Countess's life, has caused uproar amongst the upper echelons of Italian society. The Countess herself permitted a reproduction of the letter she sent to Beauderriere; here we have a letter in support of his Lordship.

Ye Olde Fetishists Leatherworks
The Old Forge, Upper Mares Bottom Buckinghamshire
Mr Hanns
Hanns, Neece & Boompadasey

Dear Mr Hanns
I was deeply alarmed to hear that the Lord Beauderriere was in some kind of trouble following his recent declaration that he is to publish a written work on the life of the Countess de Verucca.

I am a humble belt maker and worked my way to the top of my profession and I am now proud to be CEO of this establishment. Many years ago, when I was just a hands-on man on the factory floor, I had the privilege of becoming acquainted with his Lordship, who was at this time teaching biology at a ladies seminary.

Whilst lubricating a rather exquisite piece of hide, I slipped into something of a reverie, my thoughts were miles away as I gently rubbed liberal quantities of eel mucus into the divinely leathery skin. It was some moments later when I realised that his Lordship was on his knees in front of me salivating profusely.

From that day on his Lordship and I have enjoyed a particularly piquant friendship, a friendship that breaks free from the expected social and moral boundaries and is against the law in some third world countries.

Many evenings have been spent here at the leatherworks, sometimes talking, other times simply smiling. Yes, his Lordship and I have together reached the heights of ecstasy in a truly old fashioned way.

It was all good clean fun, no funny business or sex aids were necessary, just a cow, preferably dead and a sturdy bar of saddle soap. Family entertainment really. Given the intimate nature of my association with this fine upstanding fellow, I was appalled to learn that his Countess intends to sue him for defamation of character.

In recent years I have had scant contact with his Lordship as he now spends his time with the rich and famous. However, I have had the misfortune to have become acquainted with the Countess, which fills me with regret.

Following the untimely and somewhat comical death of her husband, the Countess sought refuge in England. Often in times of trouble and trauma, she returned to these shores. In the 1970's, when her corns were playing her up rotten, she spent a week recuperating in Blackpool. Then in the 1982 she fled Rome and travelled incognito to Ipswich after a liposuction experience that went tragically wrong.

When she was widowed, she came to Buckinghamshire. Her arrival went virtually unnoticed, despite the fact that she made one of her famous entrances. Lost and alone with no shoulder to cry on she found her way, by chance, to the door of the leatherworks. I invited her in, and we discovered a mutual friend in his Lordship. We chatted and drank wine; the rest is a blur. I awoke the following day lying on a floor slippery with saddle soap.

I found the Countess, unconscious and spread-eagled on the cutting table. She was wearing nothing but a studded dog collar and a self-satisfied smile. Only a totally depraved harlot of raunchy demeanour could have driven me to such depravity, and she was it. Since then, I have prayed to God every night to forgive me.

I have now returned to my innocent ways and have vowed never to shag anything that moves ever again. Lord Beauderriere once told me that some old cow would get me into trouble one day, we never thought it would be the Countess. I would like to stand up and be counted as one of his Lordship's staunchest friends. I swear that I am prepared to go down on my knees to express my absolute and unfailing support for him. I am also happy to assume that position during other activities if the price is right.
Stanley Wimbles

<<<<<<<<>>>>>>>

HUMOUR FROM THE 19th CENTURY
SERVANT: "Ma'am, your husband has eloped with the cook!"
WIFE: "Good! Now I can have the maid to myself, once in a while."

<<<<<<<<>>>>>>>

Rick Faberge's Column
"Even some thing's I don't like are expensive"

Rick Faberge shot to fame as lead singer of the 70's rock band 'Superstud Megastar'. He owns a castle in Scotland and collects expensive things. He has been married nine times to six different blondes. Rick enjoys spending money and having sex. Sometimes the two enjoyments have had to be combined.

Family or Friends - Which is best?
Well, it's obvious really, the best people to have around you are friends. I mean your family know all your little secrets and such like, whereas you can still impress your friends with your money, flash cars and big

houses. I haven't seen any of my family since I told them all to sod off and leave me alone. They were just scrounging windbags, always moaning about how granny needs a new hip, Cousin Charlie hasn't worked for years and just needs a little bit of cash to get him started self-employed and how they haven't been able to find a donor for my dad.

What the hell does he want a kebab for, his heart is weak, and a greasy one would kill him. No, it's best to stick with your friends, you know they only want you for your money, they don't try the 'we're family Ricky' rubbish on you.

Stick with your friends, at least you know where you stand.

<<<<<<<<<>>>>>>>

Kev Mugton's
Fine Art Course

Kev Mugton shot to fame after a brief appearance on TV when he famously miscut some MDF and emulsioned a 17th century marble fireplace. Kev has always been interested in painting but has no experience whatsoever.

Real Painting

Wotcha, y'know, when it all comes down to it, there's not much difference between me and all those old painters, Leonardo De Caprio, Vango, Munny and Manny and the like.

I slap emulsion on walls, and they slap paint on canvas, the only difference is that they give 'em names. I am also like that Pickarseole bloke. Firstly, I went through my own colour period, blue, sunshine yellow and green, but I must admit it was mainly magnolia. Secondly, looking at the wife, I think I married one of 'is models. Can't fink of anything else to say, might talk about something else next month tata!

<<<<<<<<<>>>>>>>

Hollywood Interviews

Each Month one of our Columnists will interview a famous Hollywood Star. This month "Zen" 'Zen' talks to Luigi Carbone, director of such films as 'The Mind Blower;' 'The Thing Under the Bed' and 'Telepathic Man'

'Zen': Welcome, if I could ask you, did you know how influential your films would be to believers such as me?

Luigi: Wotta you talk about, itsa just a films, a way to maka da big money froma da morons lika you!

'Zen': What perception! you must have some sort of sixth sense. When did you realise this?

Luigi: Wotsa all this talking sixth sense bollocks...sixth sense, I thinka you hava no bleeding sense. Ask me about my films you stupido!

'Zen': I don't believe it... fantastic, that's why I'm here... to ask you about your films, how did you know... Unbelievable!

'Zen' dropped his notes on the floor, and he crawled on his hands and knees to pick them up.

Luigi: I am a not going to sit here wiv this bleeding looney!

At this point Luigi Carbone left the room. 'Zen' returns to his chair and see Luigi's chair empty

'Zen: He's dematerialised himself, that was brilliant, I can honestly say that I have met of the foremost Masters of the Occult. Brilliant. *Suddenly all the lights go out.*

'Zen': I knew that would happen...brilliant!

<<<<<<<<>>>>>>>

Marjorie Kyte-Hopper's
Guide to Life

'Auntie' Marjorie Kyte-Hopper's career as Advisor to the World began when, as a Brownie, she started bossing people about and giving her opinions freely. Marjorie, who was married once, only briefly. She lives in Norfolk with her dog Attila Marjorie, much to her astonishment, is a gay icon.

There's Nothing Wrong In being Gay

Hello Dear Readers, I overheard some elderly ladies at the fete last week condemning the Vicar for being gay! I ask you, what could possibly be wrong with that. I interrupted and admonished them. I told them, that with so much misery in the world, it's nice when people openly admit they are gay. I am always gay,

I enjoy a good laugh and have many a merry thought. The ladies said that they shouldn't be allowed to marry each other. Preposterous! If like-minded people married each other there would be less arguments.

The ladies, eyeing me strangely, said there was also the rumour that there was at least one Lesbian in the village. I said that, although I have never been to Lesbia, I am sure they are very nice people. And as a Gay icon, people look up to me to promote merriment, laughter and gaiety.

Shout it out loud, I'm Gay and proud of it!!

<<<<<<<<<>>>>>>>>

The Cloud Cuckoo Report
In this section we try and help out people with a particular problem. One of our readers has a problem that our Review expert can help with (probably not!)

A PIG OF A PROBLEM

Reader: I run a smallholding in which I keep, amongst other livestock, five pigs. However, I'm finding them difficult to control. Despite recently installed electric fencing two of them managed to escape. One of them, the most adventurous, broke loose the other day and was discovered at the local market.

His brother, however, stayed at home. Added to this is the worry of the pig's diet; is it usual for one pig to eat roast beef while another (from the same litter) has none?

The most worrying this is that the fifth pig (also a bit of an escapologist) cries constantly when brought home from one of his jaunts. What can I do?

Expert: The best thing would be to get rid of two of the pigs and buy yourself a wolf. Make sure that is a non-smoker with a larger than average lung capacity. The remaining three pigs will soon leave home.

Reader: But where will they live?

Expert: Don't worry. One in three pigs is perfectly capable of constructing a safe and solid shelter out of durable building materials.

Reader: But what about the two other pigs?

Expert: Unfortunately, statistics show that these two pigs (I'm guessing they will be impatient by nature) are unlikely to be able to fend for themselves for long. Although they may well assemble living quarters in record time the build quality will be poor.

Reader: Why couldn't they live with their brother? The one who is capable of constructing a safe and solid shelter out of durable building materials.

Expert: Don't rush things. Allow the two impatient pigs to make their own mistakes before letting them move in with their brother.

Reader: Will their brother mind them moving in with him?

Expert: Initially he'll have reservations, particularly if his two impatient brothers had taken the Mickey out of him for his meticulous approach to building work. Eventually loneliness will dictate that he welcomes them.

Reader: What about the wolf you suggested I purchase?

Expert: Well, he will be responsible for destroying the first two pigs homes. It is highly probably that he'll track the pig's down to their brother's sturdy abode. However, even a wolf with extraordinary blowing powers will find it difficult to demolish such a well-built property.

Reader: That's a relief. But aren't the pigs going to become hermits...too afraid to leave the house because of the rampaging wolf?

Expert: Try to encourage the pigs to lure the wolf down the chimney and into a large pot of boiling water.
    It's simple and very effective way of eliminating the threat to your pigs.

Reader: Thank you so much for all your help. One last question, what will happen to the two pigs that I got rid of in the first place?

Expert: I haven't a clue. I am only au fait with three or five pig scenarios. Other porcine groups baffle me.

If you have any little problems that the Editors could help you with do not hesitate to contact us.

<<<<<<<<>>>>>>>

HUMOUR FROM THE 19th CENTURY
How were Adam and Eve kept from gambling?
Their pair of dice was taken away from them!

<<<<<<<<>>>>>>>

Millicent 1940's Wife

War is nearly over and people throughout England are looking forward to a bright new future.

"Dwarling?" said Millicent as she blacked her grate with gusto. "Would you be awfully cross if I invented something called the Dildo?" Millicent's husband Gordon toyed with the buttons on his fly and looked at his wife sensuously.

"Now Millingtony-poopsylove," he said with a kindly flick of his head, "you simply must get these silly ideas out of your head. You invent something new every month and quite frankly I find it arousing. And anyway, there's that plan of the Festival of Britain to look over and weren't you supposed to be entertaining Mrs Hartlepool's Polish friend this afternoon?" "Yes I know Dwarling." said Millicent deftly producing a script for Tommy Handley's ITMA show.

"I wasn't thinking of inventing the Dildo now!" she laughed, "I plan to wait until the late 1970's, Susan and Robert will be off our hands, so I'll have more time."

Gordon coughed and, buffing his Bakelite braces aggressively, said, "Come on old girl, let's not have any more talk of inventions. You've got to think about making some jelly for the pigs party and didn't I overhear you offering to throw the orphans out in the street?" Millicent cast her eyes downward,

"Yes Dwarling," she said sorrowfully, "but I just thought that inventing the Dildo would get us out of this hateful, hateful financial mess.

I've thought it all through, simply every woman would have one either in or on their bedside table.

Gordon removed his trousers and thrust his hands deeply into Millicent's cami-knickers. He was aroused now. "We went through all this when you had the idea of camps for people to go on holiday to.

Now let's just forget all about cloud cuckoo land ideas, you sit and hold my member, and I'll give you such a nice surprise. Millicent smiled to herself. Gordon was the most divine husband in the world. "Promise you're not awfully cross."

<<<<<<<<<>>>>>>>>

Tracy Mugton's Wedding Journal

The Editors, perhaps in a drunken stupor have asked Tracy Mugton to write about her forthcoming wedding and the necessary preparations required. Anyway, fills up a page don't it.

The Editors of The Egerton Review have asked me to write a column leading up to my wedding to Tim in July. Wiv only two months to go I'm really getting nervous. We've got the rings and the wedding cake and as you can see at the bottom of this page, I've got the dress an' all.

My future father-in-law, Lord Beauderriere, has let me take over a wing of Beauderriere Castle for me and my bridesmaids an' nat.

He often pops along as we are getting ready to go out. My friend Kylie, who is staying with me, was 'aving a shower when she turned round and saw 'is Lordship standing in the cubicle with her, stark bollock naked.

He said 'e 'ad lost 'is way cos the 'ouse is big. bleedin' liar, 'e woz just after a shag, dirty git.

I haven't seen Tim for a while, someone said he is working as an assistant to the Countess de Verucca Well I can't fink of anyfink else to say, so Tada!

<<<<<<<<<>>>>>>>>

Spot the Football Player Competition

Take part in our great new Spot the Football Player competition. Look closely at the ball and decide where you think the players are. No Prizes, just the joy of taking part

<<<<<<<<<>>>>>>>>

In the Potting Shed with Old Nobby
A Selection of Non-Motivational Quotes from our resident miserable old git!

"If you can stay calm, while all around you is chaos...then you probably haven't the faintest idea of what's happening!"

<<<<<<<<<>>>>>>>>

Letters from our Readers
The following is a selection of the boring dreary rubbish sent to us by readers of the magazine.

Dear Editors of The Egerton Review
At the risk of raising dust in the already turbulent life of the Countess de Verucca, I'd like to ask if she has a drink problem. I've noticed that she looks a little worse for wear these days. Is she prone to over-imbibing do you think?
Yours, Rupert Nanesque
Over-imbibing is all part of her job Rupert. The Editors

Dear Editors of The Egerton Review
Have you any idea when will Dorset Barrington be out of prison?
Yours, Alf Coggs
Hopefully never Alf, his column has improved since he was 'banged up.' We feel it has more grit. The Editors.

Dear Editors at The Egerton Review
Who the hell does Kev Mugton think he is?
Yours, Ferdinand Bell-Bloute
Kev has no pretensions Ferdinand; he can even spell the word. So kindly piss off Ferdy! The Editors.

Dear Editors of The Egerton Review
Is Neville Slipton a homosexual?
Yours Crispin Banyard
Not yet Crispin. The Editors.

Dear Editors of The Egerton Review
Please send my subscription money back. I am highly dissatisfied with your publication.
Yours, Miss Marigold Penny-Pincher-Prude
Unfortunately, all subscription monies are placed in the de Verucca Liquid Lunch Fund.

You are welcome to write directly to the Countess and request a refund, but you may have to resign yourself to receiving a crate of empties in lieu of your miniscule investment..

Howdy Editors of The Egerton Review
As y'all are ignoring my phone calls, I have resorted to contacting you via your letter page. Even though I suspect you we behind my recent vicious assault, I am still interested in investing in your Magazine and wish to be re-instated as the Chairman.

I have had a sort of firm to floppy offer on the farm and expect to be in the money pretty soon. Also, my Country & Western Album has entered the Top 1000 so, here's hoping.
So long, Stet Chetson
Leave us alone you tiresome pseudo-yank. The Editors.

Dear Editors of The Egerton Review
I recently got the sack because of you! I was laughing at Dorset Barrington going to prison and suffered immediate dismissal from my position at the Funeral Parlour. Could I possibly have a job at the Review? I can type and I am not at all squeamish.
Yours, Gerald Melton

We are not in need of any extra help in the office but, as you say you are not squeamish perhaps you should write to Neville Slipton as he is always saying he needs someone to give him a hand whilst dressing. The Editors.

Dear Editors of The Egerton Review
I was alarmed to hear about the horrible assault on your ex-chairman, Stet Chetson. He seems such a nice, friendly person as most Americans are.
Yours, Margaret Root

Sorry, we didn't have enough room or inclination to answer Ms Root's letter. The Editors

<<<<<<<<>>>>>>>

Classified Advertisements

Sold Out! Of Everything
Nobody wants or has anything.

Obituaries
And nobody's died lately How bloody annoying

Sorry. The Editors

<<<<<<<<>>>>>>>

The Egerton Review
Things you never wanted to know, told to you by people who know nothing about them

Vol. 1   May 2004

Stet Chetson, our ex-chairman who still hasn't sold the ranch and probably deserved the spanking he got and probably deserved a lot more. You are probably wondering why we are still showing pictures of our ex-Chairman Stet Chetson. Well, we are sure that he will continue to make a fool of himself, and we want to be there when he does.

Well, it's May and Summer is very near. We, the Editors, never take a holiday as it is our pride and purpose to get regular editions of the Review out there for our readers. So, what's in this month's Egerton Review, well, usual load of old bollocks I suppose. This month, Neville Slipton is overjoyed because he has a new assistant, and he has also interviewed an Hollywood star.

Dorset Barrington is still in prison and getting on well with his new 'friend' 'Thruster.' Rick Faberge has been interviewed by the police after he attended a May Day gathering on the South Coast. Apparently, the May Pole he asked the young ladies to dance around was not fixed in the ground but protruding from his trousers.

Tracy Mugton's Wedding Journal is another 'gem' in the Crown we like to call The Egerton Review. Read and Enjoy, that's an order. The Editors.

<<<<<<<<>>>>>>>

Darcy Copperfield's
Literature Unleashed

At the tender age of ten Darcy Copperfield was expelled from St. Peregrine's School for Boys for writing 'Anne of Green Gables is a nymphomaniac' on the blackboard. How times have changed, nowadays Copperfield's observations about sex and perversion in literature are respected and salivated over worldwide..

Sir Arthur Conan the Barbarian

Imagine, if you will, a cold winters evening, with the rain lashing the windows of 221b Baker Street. Sitting in front of a roaring fire is the renowned Consultant Detective Sherlock Holmes, opposite him sits his faithful companion and cocaine supplier, Dr. Watson.

These two men have spent too long alone in each other's company to be just good friends. I mean, it is well documented that Holmes had an aversion to women. He surrounded himself with men, Watson, Lestrade and, of course, Professor Moriarty.

And look at some of the titles of his 'Adventures;' 'The Man with the Twisted Lip; The Noble Bachelor; The Engineer's Thumb and the Adventure of the Second Stain. I rest my case. But the worst thing of all were his adventures with what he called his 'Baker Street Irregulars.' These were young boys who would do things for him for a shilling or two. He was always looking at things through his magnifying glass and sucking on his Meerschaum. Very strange indeed, don't you think.

COULD YOU WRITE EROTIC FICTION?

Send your exotic fantasies, in the form of a short story, to Darcy Copperfield c/o The Egerton Review for use in any other edition of the Review or for Darcy's personal files. Please include a photograph of yourself. Sorry we can't return submissions.

<<<<<<<<>>>>>>>

Text Message From History

I saw Queen Elizabeth 1 addressing her troops at Tilbury before they set off to fight the Spanish Armada; "I may have the body of a weak and feeble woman; but I have the heart and stomach of Dame Judi Dench!" #gogetthem

<<<<<<<<<>>>>>>>

Neville Slipton's
Language Workshop
"My tongue is my passport"

Neville Slipton was born Susan Grace Sliptonova in 1956. His deep interest in, and unrivalled grasp of, languages stemmed from living in a multi-lingual environment in no less than forty-three countries.

Getting Personal With A Dresser

Last month one of our readers wrote in asking to become my personal dresser/companion. The application couldn't have been better timed because, *mon boeuf bourguignon*, I have recently sprained my wrist and am unable to pop my mules on unassisted.

Enter Gerald Melton, an absolute darling of a man whose recent dismissal from the funeral parlour, he had worked there as make-up artiste for many years, was a tragedy. But as one door closes another *Porte oeuvres* as they say.

Since the interview Gerald and I have been literally inseparable. He's a complete and utter dream, always ready with a smile, a helping hand and some people think of everything, a pot of Vaseline.

A must for lubricating the bits of you that travel can make weary. So, this month's column is dedicated to Gerald without whom I would be stark naked all of the time instead of some of the time. For those of you who aren't precious enough to merit the attention of a personal dresser allow me to elucidate. A personal dresser is responsible for ensuring that his master is constantly immaculate.

Gerald, for example, never leaves the chateau without a needle and thread; several newly pressed *items de chiffon* and a Dorothy bag filled to the brim with Estée Lauder accoutrements. We're having so much fun together Melty (my little pet name for him) and I and hope that you will join us on our travels around the globe. Below, a useful phrase. Try it.

"Poochkins, could you be an absolute sweetie and slip that in there....ooh lovely, now close the suitcase. (my little pet name again)"

I haven't included a foreign translation for the above phrase. It simply doesn't come across right. So, in the event that your personal dresser is foreign simply remember that actions speak louder than words.

<<<<<<<<<>>>>>>>

at home with...
The Beauderriere's

Lord Beauderriere, in his ignorance, believes that the general viewing public is chomping at the bit to hear of the exploits of this dissolute excuse for an aristocrat. To our eyes, it's just a feeble ruse to relive his salad days. He prefers to use this picture of himself. We don't know why, nor do we care, as any picture of him now would scare the horses and small children.

A SCRIPT FOR TELEVISION

EPISODE 5: LORD BEAUDERRIERE AND HIS GARDENER

SCENE 1 (IN WHICH LORD BEAUDERRIERE IS FIRMER AND HARDER)

CAST:
LORD B - A FAT ARISTOCRAT
PLUMM   - LORD B'S GARDENER

INT: LORD BEAUDERRIERE'S GREENHOUSE

LORD B. IS SITTING, HIS BUTTOCKS STRAINING, IN A TATTERED WICKER CHAIR.

LORD BEAUDERRIERE:
I say, Plummy, how about using this for a dibber?

PLUMM:
I don't think it's big enuff zur!

LORD BEAUDERRIERE:
I'm very rich and important you snivelling horticulturist. Take this in your hand or I'll report you to the Alan Titchmarsh.

PLUMM:
It might do to prick out, my Lord

LORD BEAUDERRIERE:
Plummy, it's not prick out, that I had in mind!

In the next issue Lord Beauderriere talks to his Gardener

<<<<<<<<>>>>>>>

Countess de Verucca's
Liquid Lunch

The Countess lives in Monaco and regularly campaigns for the abolition of alcohol-free beverages. We apologise for the appalling transcript, but the Countess gave us her column early one morning after a night on the booze on our rather old answering machine, we have done our best.

There doesn't seem to be anything on the ansaphone from the Countess this time. All we could hear was a clatter of bottles, a lot of cursing and what appears to be the sound of someone tumbling down the stairs. Nothing to worry about I expect, perhaps we will hear from her at a later date. **The Editors.**

<<<<<<<<<>>>>>>>>

'Zen' Sven's
Sphere of Enigma

'Zen' Sven was born in the Scandinavian quarter of Ipswich. He has been obsessed by the paranormal since taking LSD at school and considers himself an impartial investigator. 'Zen' became a Vegan after accidentally eating a pit-bull terrier while in a meditative trance. "I mistook it for an ectoplasmic grill-steak." confesses 'Zen.' "Since then, I haven't eaten meat at all and I'm always careful to remove weevils from the vegetables I do it. 'Zen's' hobbies include contacting the dead. "They're so interesting."

Crop Circles

It was midnight when I arrived outside the sleepy village of Lower Undercarriage. Across the wide expanse of cornfields, I could see flashing lights and I could hear faint, unearthly noises.

I ventured nearer and stumbled across someone else interested in what was obviously, the making of crop circles by beings not of this world. "Look where yer soddin' going, yer big tit!' said my new companion. I had evidently taken him by surprise. I introduced myself and refused a swig from his can of Special Brew. I asked him if he had seen the being that were causing the crop circles. "Yes," he said, "it's them bleedin' tossers from the next vi..."

"Galaxy!" I interrupted. "If yer like," he said and mumbled something about one being born every minute, This man was a fount of knowledge, not only did he know the home galaxy of these beings, he also knew the gestation period of its females.

We watched the flashing light and listened to the strange noises for another thirty minutes and then everything went dark and quiet. A little while later we both stood up and my companion, who seemed a little unsteady on his feet, collapsed to the ground again.

I left him and made my way to the site of the crop circles. The ground was covered with strange geometric shapes and the whole area had a strange unearthly aroma I took photographs and walked back to my companion. With him were three other people, all rather unsteady on their feet, but generous enough to offer me swigs from their Special Brew cans and to tell me that I was their best mate. Such is the camaraderie amongst those whose minds are on a higher plane. I offered them a lift into the village which they gladly accepted. They were a jovial bunch, each time my friend mumbled something to them, they all burst out laughing and pointing at me. We stopped in the village and my passengers all got out, they moved off fortified by their beer and the £20 note I had given them. Next morning I found the rear seats of my caravanette covered with corn ears and straw and I could detect the faint aroma I had smelt in the cornfield. The man at the valet cleaning company said the smell was a combination of piss and vomit, I think not. I believe that I had an encounter with beings from a galaxy far, far away.

<<<<<<<<<>>>>>>>>

Witty Man
'He has an answer for ~~everything~~ nothing'

We have been informed that Witty Man has gone on holiday. Let us hope he will spend his unpaid leave at the Museum of Witticisms in Lower Undercarriage.

Dr. Makitupp Azugoalong's
Quick Clinic

All too aware that medical jargon and detailed diagnoses can worry patients, Dr Azugoalong, an Iron Maiden fan, set up the first on-line East European Monosyllabic Medical Response Clinic in 1998. Dr Azugoalong speaks very little English.

Dear Doctor Azugoalong,
I'm a linguist, does it necessarily follow that I might be bi-lingual?
Yes.

Dear Doctor Azugoalong,
I recently got trapped in a lavatory with a wildebeest. It was terrifying. I often refer to the incident as the Gnu Loo Saga which is, funnily enough, an anagram of your surname. Did you know that?
Yes.

Dear Doctor Azugoalong,
I'm in prison and I'm getting a funny little rash. I've tried asking my friend 'Thruster' if he has a funny little rash, but he just gets sulky. Is there an ointment available?
Yes.

Dear Doctor Azugoalong,
I'm worried about my cellmate who has a funny little rash. Is there any ointment available?
No.

Dear Doctor Azugoalong,
My name is Rupert Nanesque and I'm thinking of becoming a ballet dancer, do you think I have the legs for it? I enclose a pair of my most recently worn support tights for examination.
Left leg YES. Right leg NO.

Dear Doctor Azugoalong,
I haven't started wearing a bra yet. Is that normal?
Yes.

Dear Doctor Azugoalong,
I keep thinking people are Norwegian. Am I Norwegian...I mean normal?
No.

<<<<<<<<>>>>>>>

Text Message From History
Texting from Bosworth Field 22-8-1485
It's been really noisy here, and then I heard King Richard the Third shout, I'm hoarse, I'm hoarse, my kingdom for a throat sweet. I think!

<<<<<<<<>>>>>>>

Public Eye
your observations appreciated

doppelgangers
We invite you to send in examples of look-alikes. Only the most astounding resemblances with be published.

Arthur Herring observes.
My pet hamster (pictured) looks identical to that man you keep putting in doppelgangers who doesn't look like anything remotely human What do the readers think?

children say the funniest things

Janet Monks shares this with us:
My daughter Bethany didn't want to go to bed one night. When I told her that she must go to bed to get her beauty sleep she said, "No

mummmeeee leave me alone you bitch I hate you I want a drink of water aggggghh don't smack me mummy please I'll phone ChildLine if you ever leave burn marks again..." **How we laughed!**

Yes, yes, I know we used this same thing before. As it was a couple of months ago we didn't think you'd notice.

<<<<<<<<<>>>>>>>>

"you'll never guess who I saw..."

Mrs. Irma Liarr spotted: **Frankenstein's Monster** at a Betty Ford Clinic (Croydon Branch)
"I was surprised to see him there, as I though was just made up! I also didn't know he had drink problem."

<<<<<<<<<>>>>>>>>

Rick Faberge's Column
"Even things I don't like are expensive"

Rick Faberge shot to fame as lead singer of the 70's rock band 'Superstud Megastar'. He owns a castle in Scotland and collects expensive things. He has been married nine times to six different blondes. Rick enjoys spending money and having sex. Sometimes the two pleasures have had to be combined.

St Tropez? - St Leonards? Which is best?
Rick Faberge Investigates

I'm sure that around about now you're planning your holidays. You get two weeks off of work and want to enjoy yourselves. For me, life is just one long holiday, that's because I am filthy rich, and you aren't. You spend the evenings scanning brochures for that ideal spot to spend your meagre savings on. I, on the other hand, can just jump in my personal jet and fly off to any one of my many homes worldwide.

I suppose you have no choice really, whereas I have a great deal of choice, but it can just as frustrating for me as it is for you; where do I go, Biarritz. St. Tropez or take my yacht through the Med....so much choice. You don't know how lucky you are!

<<<<<<<<<>>>>>>>>

Kev Mugton's
Fine Art Course

Kev Mugton shot to fame after a brief appearance on TV when he famously miscut some MDF and emulsioned a 17th century marble fireplace. Kev has always been interested in painting but has no experience whatsoever. Kev hopes to win the Turner Prize one day, and let's face it, there's no reason why he shouldn't. Kev also hopes to win the Mastermind Rose Bowl too but that's unlikely as he is fundamentally thick as two miscut planks.

Ming or Mugton: Can you tell the difference?

Wotcha, I started going to pottery classes so I could make something for Tracy and Tim's wedding. I thought that they wouldn't want me to spend a lot of money on something fancy. So, I decided to make them a Ming vase. As I made the vase, I wondered how all of them people long ago made things out of pottery when there were no night classes to go to. When I had finished, I reckon no one could've told the difference between mine and one of that bloke Ming's. I proudly showed it to Tracy, and she sat there looking at it for a long time, sobbing. I think she loved it.

<<<<<<<<<>>>>>>>>

Marjorie Kyte-Hopper's
Guide to Life

'Auntie' Marjorie Kyte-Hopper's career as Advisor to the World began when, as a Brownie, she started bossing people about and giving her opinions freely. Marjorie, who was married once, only briefly , recently published a book, 'Country Looks for the Woolly-Haired.' She lives in Norfolk with her dog Attila. Marjorie, much to her astonishment, is a gay icon.

Cottaging In The Village

Hello Dear Readers, I was thumbing through my copy of *People's Friend* the other day, when I heard a knock on the door. I opened it to find my next door neighbour Major Brashe. He was in a very agitated state. He said that he had received a summons from the courts to face a charge of cottaging.

I sat him down and poured him a generous glass of Wincarnis and tried to give him some sage advice. I told him that there was nothing wrong with living in a cottage, I myself had been cottaging for many years and have never been summoned before the courts.

The Major looked at me strangely and asked me if I had something stronger to drink, I went to my secret cupboard and opened a vintage bottle of Sanatogen Tonic Wine and offered him a glass. He downed it in one and asked for another.

I said that I hoped he hadn't had any alterations down to his cottage without referring them to the parish council because they can get quite obdurate. He mentioned he was being summoned for loitering around the public toilets in the village.

I told him that the government gives grants to put conveniences in Grade 1 Listed buildings, so he would have no need to use the public ones. I told him I had seen him near the public toilets in the company of the vicar, perhaps he could give him a hand. The major laughed hysterically and left. I find it so heart-warming when I can help a fellow human being in distress. *Yours, Auntie Marjorie.*

<<<<<<<<<>>>>>>>
Dorset Barrington's
Antique ~~Dealing~~ Stealing

Dorset Barrington's interest in becoming an antique dealer was inflamed by the vast amount of profit he made from selling off various priceless family heirlooms as a child. Barrington, the husband of the now penniless Lady Valkyrie Beauderriere-Barrington, makes regular appearances on 'Crimewatch' and is most famous for his popular daytime television programme 'The Three Auctioneers.' He is now residing at Her Majesty's Pleasure in HMP Grymthorpe.

Hello lovers of fine art, as you are now well aware, I am residing at Her Majesty's Pleasure in the maximum security wing of HMP Cleckhampton situated on the wildest of moors in some place called 'The North.'

This prison has all the comforts of home, if one was used to eating shit, pissing in a bucket and showering with 25 other men. I can assure you that I have never eaten shit or pissed in a bucket.

My only contact with the antiques world is my regular copy of 'Antiques are only for Poofs,' a magazine written on toilet roll with orange crayon by my cell-mate 'Thruster.' From this I have gleaned that Formica is the new oak and that he, 'Thruster' could make a better Ming vase in the pottery workshop.

I can only look forward to my release date. Brighter things are on the horizon, I have been chosen to be Soap Picker Up in the showers next month.

'Thruster' says I should think myself lucky to have been chosen. He said that I will be up against stiff competition to hold my position the following month. Oh well. Hey Ho for now. Tip: Keep looking out for Arthur Maudsleydale Inventions.

<<<<<<<<>>>>>>>

HUMOUR FROM THE 19th CENTURY
What can you fill a barrel with to make it lighter?
HOLES!

Text Message From History
The generals are sitting around a table, Napoleon stands. "Ok, Ok, that's settled then, Wellington gets the rubber boots, and I get the brandy, seems fair to me!" #gotthebest

<<<<<<<<>>>>>>>

Millicent 1940's Wife
War is nearly over and people throughout England are looking forward to a bright new future.

"Dwarling?" said Millicent sewing a reinforcing patch into the gusset of her camiknickers. "Would you be awfully cross if I invented something called dishwasher?" Millicent's husband Gordon put down his Bakelite whittling knife and looked at his wife askance.

"Now Millie," he said with a kindly smile, "you simply must get these daft ideas out of your head. I know it's exciting inventing things but it's really men's work and you're unlikely to make any money. And anyway, there are the church bells to be cleaned with Brasso and that Air raid shelter won't dismantle itself!

"Yes I know Dwarling." said Millicent quickly toting up the points in her ration book.

"I wasn't thinking of inventing dishwasher now!" she laughed, "I plan to wait until the 1950's, after all Susan and Robert will be grown up by then so I'll have more dishes to wash." Gordon smiled and, polishing his Bakelite pipe holder, said, "Come on you old dafty, let's not have any more talk of inventions. You've got to think about making that tripe pie for supper and didn't I overhear you offering to pleasure old Mr. Harrison, it has been quite a while since last time.

Millicent bowed her head, "Yes Dwarling," she said mournfully, "but I just thought that inventing the dishwasher would get us out of this awful financial mess. I've thought it all through. Just think of all the free time a housewife will have if they are not forever at the sink!"

Gordon adjusted his truss and stood up. His hands grasped flowers in a nearby vase and crushing them. He was angry now. "We went through all this when you had that soppy idea about calculating machines you carry around in your pocket.

Now let's just forget all about these crazy-arsed schemes, you sit down and carry on darning your underwear and I'll get us a Carr's Water Biscuit to share, shall I?" Millicent smiled to herself. Gordon was a simply marvellous husband, "Promise you're not awfully cross Dwarling." she pleaded.

<<<<<<<<<>>>>>>>>

Hollywood Interviews

Each Month one of our Columnists will interview a famous Hollywood Star. This month Kev Mugton talks to Gustav Heckler, Oscar winning Set Designer of such films as: 'The Minimalist;' 'The Bare Room' and 'The Day After The Bailiff's Came'

Kev: Well, it's smashing to meet you. Have you always been interested in design. How old were you when you realised design was for you?

Gustav: Nein! I was not...

Kev:	Since you were nine years old, blimey! I didn't become interested 'til my Tracy was born. 'Ad to do up her nursery, realised I 'ad a flair.
Gustav:	Scheiße Kopf! Vot is das! Dummkopf!!
Kev:	Thanks, yeah, I'm a sorta designer meself, but I use the mediums of paint and MDF.
Gustav:	Gott in Teufel!!
Kev:	Nah, got it in B&Q
Gustav:	Mein films ve should discuss!
Kev:	Yeah, can't say I ever saw them at the pictures.
Gustav:	Vell, nein, zay were vot you call, Cult Classics, Film Noir, Art House Studies, umm.
Kev:	Straight to video eh, shame.
Gustav:	Do you do ceilings?
Kev:	Yeah, I could sort you out an estimate

Well at least Kev got something out of it.

<<<<<<<<>>>>>>>

Tracy Mugton's Wedding Journal

The Editors, perhaps in a drunken stupor have asked Tracy Mugton to write about her forthcoming wedding and the necessary preparations required. Anyway, fills up a page doesn't it.

Only 2 mumfs to go now, can't wait, soon I'll be Mrs. Short-Cummins. I still haven't seen Tim for a while, he must still be working for that piss-head Countess. Although, I think he paid me a secret visit the other night. It was about 2 in the morning when my bedroom door opened, and a shadowy figure of a man crept slowly to the end of my bed. He raised the bedclothes at the bottom and gradually crawled up the bed. Well, I don't have to tell you girls, he did things that made me go a little red, and not to say, a little sore. I whispered in his ear as he was plundering my inner warmth with his massive member, "Can you stay all night?."

A voice murmured that I mustn't ask his questions like that, or he'll report me to Ann Summers. He left as soon as he came and I was lying on the bed, well and truly shagged. It must have been my Timmy, only my Timmy would have gone where that mystery figure went on that rather exciting night. See yer next month.

<<<<<<<<>>>>>>>

In the Potting Shed with Old Nobby
A Selection of Non-Motivational Quotes from our resident miserable old git!

"Always be yourself because I'm pretty positive no other bugger wants to be YOU!"

<<<<<<<<>>>>>>>

Letters from our Readers
The following is a selection of the boring dreary rubbish sent to us by readers of the magazine.

Dear Editors at The Egerton Review,
Margaret Root, who wrote to you last month, must be a deranged old bat if she honestly believes that Stet Chetson is a REAL American. It's pathetic.
Norma Westfield

Kindly resist the urge to slag off The Egerton Review readers Ms. Westfield. That's our job. The Editors

Dear Editors at The Egerton Review,
When am I due to be released from prison?
Dorset Barrington
Dunno mate. Just keep emailing the column. It's a great success. The Editors

Dear Editors at The Egerton Review,
Does Ferdinand Bell-Bloute reckon himself or what?
Kev Mugton
We don't want to cause any trouble Kev but yes, we think he does reckon himself. He's constantly slagging you off and even tried to get off with your wife last week at the social club. The Editors

Dear Editors at The Egerton Review,
Has Neville Slipton come out of the closet yet?
Crispin Banyard
Not to our knowledge. Mind you, it is a walk-in closet and he's usually in there with Gerald Melton. The Editors

Howdy Editors at The Egerton Review,
I have the distinct feeling that you guys at The Egerton Review are laughing at me. I wanna know why.
Stet Chetson
Because you are an object of ridicule Stet! The Editors.

Dear Editors at The Egerton Review,
I had to write to inform you that the Countess de Verucca gave me the much-prized Alfa Romeo Tiara (fashioned from resin and real diamante) as recompense for the money I unwisely spent on a subscription to your dreadful, debauched and blasphemous publication. She is clearly a marvellous woman, nothing like the drunken muck-bucket you claim she is.
Miss Marigold Penny-Pincher-Prude
ell, isn't that nice? Suggestion: Look up the meanings of the following words: marvellous, dreadful, debauched, blasphemous. The OED should enlighten. The Editors.

Dear Editors at The Egerton Review,
I recently took a job as Neville Slipton's personal dresser but find I am constantly exhausted. Should I quit?
Gerald Melton
Please don't. We think he's in love with you and dread having to deal with him if he gets dumped. The Editors.

<<<<<<<<>>>>>>>>

Classified Advertisements

HOW TO SEX A BOA CONSTRICTOR
A necessary handbook for breeding Boas £3.99

How to have Sex with a Boa Constrictor. Step by step guide to wooing and finally getting your end away. £15.00

FOR SALE I was a Teenage Boa Constrictor Porn Star. Video £9.99

Psychic Readings by 'Zen' Sven. Call The Review.

Free toilet roll paper, tubes were sold to collector. Pop in any time with lots of bags.

Handbag size metal effect Gentleman's Gun, never used at night, 25 guineas.

Countess de Verucca Book of Wines. Indecipherable £15.99

Unsigned, unused, unwanted copy of Big Ranchman Sings Country (by Stet Chetson). £5.00

I don't have anything to sell I am just lonely. Oh, bugger, perhaps I should have put this in the Personal Column.

<<<<<<<<>>>>>>>>

Wanted – Domestic Staff.

Single gentleman is looking for experienced staff to work in his home. He requires One or two to buckle his shoe; three or four to knock at the door; five or six to pick up sticks, seven or eight to close the gate and nine or ten to tend his large obese rooster. Please send photo.

PERSONAL

<u>Bachelor, handsome early 30's millionaire</u> doesn't need to meet anyone. He has to beat them off with a stick.

<u>Lovely, lonely old woman</u> would like to meet up with lovely old man with a view to...to...umm... Hello are you my mother.

<<<<<<<<>>>>>>>

For Sale
1 Large Boa Constrictor Slightly Abused

<<<<<<<<>>>>>>>

The Egerton Review is finally sponsored by: Matron Small's Rose Tinted Glasses

CAUTION: May impair vision, wearers may become susceptible to headaches etc. etc. etc.

<<<<<<<<>>>>>>>

Ye olde quaint advertisement for your delectation
The Most Sovereign Contraption

Arthur Maudsleydale's
The Stealth Cooker
A Culinary breakthrough in Silent Cooking

Banish the sounds and smells of cooking that come from kitchens. Suitable for the less well-off whose kitchen is less than 100 yards from the living area.

<<<<<<<<>>>>>>>

The Egerton Review

Things you never wanted to know, told to you by people who know nothing about them

Vol. 1   June 2004

Stet Chetson, ex-chairman and object of ridicule

June is busting out all over, so the song goes. Well, the only June we know who is busting out all over is Fat June in our office. She spends most of the day shoving jam doughnuts down her ever open gullet and covering every surface with sugar. But we love her.

She makes the rest of us fat losers look slim and lithe and athletic. Well, what can you expect from this month's load of drivel. Tracy Mugton is still banging on about her bleeding wedding.

Dorset is still banged up, in more than one way by know. Darcy is twittering on about something literary as though anybody cares.

Neville? well who cares. Kev? We're not even going to bother. I need a holiday.

We've been stuck in this bloody office for ages now. Look, if you want to know what's in this month's edition, bloody well open the book!! God, some people!!

<<<<<<<<>>>>>>>

Darcy Copperfield's
Literature Unleashed

At the tender age of ten Darcy Copperfield was expelled from St. Peregrine's School for Boys for writing 'Anne of Green Gables is a nymphomaniac' on the blackboard. How times have changed, nowadays Copperfield's observations about sex and perversion in literature are respected and salivated over worldwide.

Top Shelf Magazines, How Good Are They

I spend a lot of my time scanning the top shelfs of newsagents for the more interesting 'Gentleman's Magazines.' I'm not into those that just tantalize or suggest, I like the really good ones, those that show everything...everything! Y'know, the ones that are sealed so the casual browser can't get a free peek. If I can't see what's inside and do not really want to purchase the items, I am a revered Literary Critic y'know, I get a torch and shine along the pages, and if it's just right you can glimpse a little bit of flesh...flesh. Oh, my left arm is going a little numb and a bit of a pain in my chest, anyway, you can get a good look and with my imagination....! It was at this juncture when we, the Commissioning Editors heard a crash coming from Darcy's office. We broke down the door (*he locks it for some reason when he is writing his column*) and found Darcy slumped in a pile on the floor obviously in distress. We summoned an ambulance, and Darcy was whisked off to a special unit that the emergency people seemed to know about (you'd think that they had handled a problem like this with Darcy before). We will keep you advised as to his welfare as we hear it. The Editors.

COULD YOU WRITE EROTIC FICTION?
Send your exotic fantasies, in the form of a short story, to Darcy Copperfield c/o The Egerton Review for use in any other edition of the Review or for Darcy's personal files. Please include a photograph of yourself. Sorry we can't return submissions.

Neville Slipton's
Language Workshop
"My tongue is my passport"

Neville Slipton was born Susan Grace Sliptonova in 1956. His deep interest in, and unrivalled grasp of, languages stemmed from living in a multi-lingual environment in no less than forty-three countries. He is never happier than when he is able to use his talent with his tongue in any corner of the world.

Happy, Happy, So Happy

I am the most happiest of *'hommes'* ever since Melty came to work for me. He is always eager to pleased me and will bend over backwards and sometimes forwards to accommodate me.

I haven't been anywhere this month as I thought it best that I show Melty the ropes... and the chains and the leather suits. Many an evening is spent in discussion of all sorts of topics from holidays to me and...well, that's about it really.

I have also spent some time showing Melty my little foibles and idiosyncrasies. I have also been teaching him some foreign phrases that will help him when we go abroad. I'm afraid I am very strict with him and sometimes I have to give him a severe tongue-lashing which leaves us both rather spent and exhausted. He has told me about his time as a funeral director and I have got him to show me how he prepares bodies, how he undresses them, and washes them, makes them look good and also how he deals with the bodies when they are stiff.

I have given him some good advice about relieving stiffness in bodies. I am worried about Melty, he seems rather listless, perhaps he can shake that off when we go away.

<<<<<<<<>>>>>>>

at home with....
The Beauderrieres

Lord Beauderriere, in his ignorance, believes that the general viewing public is chomping at the bit to hear of the exploits of this dissolute excuse for an aristocrat. To my eyes, it's just a feeble ruse to relive his salad days. He prefers to use a picture of himself in his younger days as any picture of him now would scare the horses and small children

A SCRIPT FOR TELEVISION

EPISODE 6: LORD BEAUDERRIERE AND HIS AU-PAIR

SCENE 1 (IN WHICH LORD BEAUDERRIERE IS FIRM AND HARD AND ERECT)

CAST: LORD B - A FAT ARISTOCRAT
ASTRID - LORD B'S SWEDISH AU PAIR

INT: LORD BEAUDERRIERE'S STUDY

LORD B. IS SITTING, HIS BUTTOCKS STRAINING, IN A TATTERED WICKER CHAIR.

LORD BEAUDERRIERE:
I say, Astrid How about one of your special massages with extras?

ASTRID:
I don't do that sort of thing my lord, a where's the 'little fellow' you employed me to look after?

LORD BEAUDERRIERE:
I'm very rich and important you snivelling Scandinavian. Grab me 'little fellow' here or I'll put you on the next plane to Swindon!

ASTRID:
I come from Sweden, not Swindon, my Lord

LORD BEAUDERRIERE:
I know, do you know the cost of flights to Sweden?

In the next issue Lord Beauderriere and Tracy Mugton

<<<<<<<<>>>>>>>>

Countess de Verucca's
Liquid Lunch

The Countess lives in Monaco and regularly campaigns for the abolition of alcohol-free beverages.

We apologise for the appalling transcript, but the Countess gave us her column early one morning after a night on the booze on our rather old answering machine, we have done our best. The more anal readers amongst will realise that following is a copy of an earlier transcript. We decided that it doesn't matter as nobody reads her column anyway and we still haven't heard from her.

Something about Drink and Drinking
Duis autem vel eum iriure dolor in hendrerit in Chateau Neuf de Pap vulputate esse consequat, vel illum prefer Blue Nun dolore eu feugiat cheaper nulla facilisis at very pissed eros et velit esse molestie consequat bottle o' vino, wet me knickers.

Vel illum room spinning arounda null aiusto odio not responsible for my actions dig nissum. Duis autem vel Australian wines eum iriure dolore in £2.99 hendrerit in vulputate velit esse Tesco consequat, vel 90% proof and no less, vel illum dolore eu feugiat nulla facilisis eros et accumsan et hendrerit in vulputate velit esse molestie consequat. Vel illum null aiusto odio pissed outa my head dig nissum.

Duis Cabernet Sauvignon, Valpolicella autem vel eum iriure Martini Bianco sed diam nonummy dolore in drunk hendrerit Duis autem vel eum iriure consequat, vel fall over ex garden party. Duis autem vel eum iriure dolor in bucket of Claret hendrerit in vulputate esse consequat, vel illum sleep dolore eu feugiat. Duis autem vel eum iriure dolor in hendrerit in vulputate 20 litres Bull's Blood at hungover esse consequat, vel illum dolore eu surprised the Queen feugiat cheaper nulla Marguaritas facilisis lush eros et accumsan et shag anything in vulputate velit esse molestie consequat.

Vel illum boozer null aiusto odio dig nissum. Duis autem Barolo, Rioja, Chardonnay, Chablis vel smashed offa my face eum by the glass iriure dolore in entire bottle hendrerit pissed outa my brains.

<<<<<<<<>>>>>>>

'Zen' Sven's
Sphere of Enigma

Note for readers. Unlike our other columnists 'Zen' Sven declined to be photographed. He believes that a visual image of him might detract from the serious and fascinating nature of his column, we actually believe it is because he is so devastatingly ugly that no one would ever believe a word he says.

Invisibility

Whilst sitting at the breakfast table I read a letter that made me put my egg spoon down in surprise. The letter was from a friend of mine, Dicken Dalrymple. The missive informed me that strange goings on were happening in the tiny village of Lower Undercarriage in Cornwall.

This revelation was no surprise to me because I have investigated many a phenomena in this village. It seems to me that Lower Undercarriage must be a cosmic crossroads of the universe. I motored down the following day. I parked my caravanette in the pub carpark and made my way into the village. The whole place was deserted, yet I had the feeling that I was being watched.

As I walked through the village, I came across Dicken Dalrymple half in and half out of a horse trough. If the trough had been full of water, he might have drowned, and the world would have lost one of its greatest mystics.

I pulled him upright and sat him down on a nearby bench, as he seemed unsteady on his feet. I offered him a sip of diluted fruit juice from my vacuum flask, but he seemed to prefer a swig from his can of Special Brew. He looked up at me and said,

"They've all gone, yet, somehow, they're still here. They're invisible!" I looked around and he was right, the place was devoid of people, but as I scanned the area, I could see the odd twitching of curtains and sudden closing of doors. I turned to Dicken.

"When did this all start?" He took another swig from his can. "Last night there was a fog," he began. I thought to myself, 'Classic, fog, disappearances.' He continued. "Just after the pub shut, I wandered through the village, just me and my shotgun. In the murky shadows I saw strange misshapen figures.

It was obvious to me that beings from another world have used the fog as cover for an invasion. I started to shout at them and started shooting into dark corners where I thought I saw them cowering.

The villagers ran around screaming and then they...disappeared. They've all gone to another dimension, yet, somehow, they're still here." I patted him on the shoulder, placed a £20 note in his top pocket, turned, and made my way out of the village. I left behind a mystery that may never be solved.

<<<<<<<<>>>>>>>

Witty Man
'He has an answer for everything'
I...I..., we...we... oh sod it, can't be arsed to give you a reason. I can't really see this bloody magazine lasted much longer!

<<<<<<<<>>>>>>>

Dr. Makitupp Azugoalong's
Quick Clinic

All too aware that medical jargon and detailed diagnoses can worry patients, Dr Azugoalong, an Iron Maiden fan, set up the first on-line Monosyllabic Medical Response Clinic in 1998. Since then, he had longed to appear on the Jonathan Ross show and been asked to judge several pub quizzes in Birmingham. Dr Azugoalong speaks very little English.

Dear Doctor Azugoalong,
You recommended some ointment in your column last month. Could you tell me the name of it please.
No.
*NOTE: Dr Azugoalong is unable to pronounce the name of the ointment as it contains more than one syllable. Sorry. The Editors

Dear Doctor Azugoalong,
I also like listening to the tunes of Iron Maiden. Do you think we are spiritually linked in some way?
Yes.

Dear Doctor Azugoalong,
What does your name mean? Is there some kind of message in it?
No.

Dear Doctor Azugoalong,
You may recall that I wrote to you in January to tell you that I had developed an aversion to sausages and raw egg white. This dislike started shortly after you used your 'so called tongue depressor' on me.

You said I was normal when I asked you, but I now believe I am pregnant and that you are the father. Am I right in thinking that you will be making regular maintenance payments?
No.

Dear Doctor Azugoalong,
Is there a special ointment I can use to make me look younger than I am?
Yes.

Dear Doctor Azugoalong,
My mother said you are older than you look. Is it true?
Yes.

Please remember that Dr. Azugoalong is NOT a Proctologist despite his shadowy intentions

<<<<<<<<<>>>>>>>>

Rick Faberge's Column
"Even things I don't like are expensive"

Rick Faberge shot to fame as lead singer of the 70's rock band 'Superstud Megastar'. He owns a castle in Scotland and collects expensive things. He has been married nine times to six different blondes. Rick enjoys spending money and having sex. Sometimes the two enjoyments have had to be combined.

Bentley – Old Banger

Ok, so you're cruising down Rodeo Drive, eying up the ladies, you toot your horn, a rather attractive young lady turns and sees you sitting in a 1966 VW Caravanette, you will never get a shag.

Ok, so you're cruising down Rodeo Drive, eying up the ladies, you toot your horn, a rather attractive young lady turns and sees you sitting in a Bentley Mulsanne Turbo. She leaps on you and shags your brains out. Bentley or Old banger – you work it out!

<<<<<<<<<>>>>>>>>

As Kev Mugton is away on his holidays painting in the Cotswolds, or perhaps I should explain painting and decorating in the Cotswolds that we have inveigled an old maiden aunt to give a good old-fashioned recipe.

So, for the first time and may well be the last as she is getting on a bit. She's a little stuck in her ways so accept her 'old-time' attitude to life. So without more adore and I'm not just writing this to fill a page, may see introduce to you......

<<<<<<<<>>>>>>>

Cooking with Fanny
Aunt Fanny Antrobus gives us the benefit of her experiencing creating nourishing meals during the Second World War

"Feeding ones family during the Second World War was one of the hardest jobs around...I mean apart from fighting, working in Munitions Factories, fire-fighting, bomb disposal and quite a lot of other jobs really, but preparing meals using rations was very difficult.

Difficult, that is if you didn't use those nice gentlemen down the Black Market. Sod Digging for Victory, Brawn, and Pig's Heads, for an extra few pounds you could eat like Kings and Queens....I've just been handed a note by the Commissioning Editors, ...excuse me....oh. apparently, this isn't the sort of Wartime Survival Guide they wanted...Tata! Arseholes!"

<<<<<<<<>>>>>>>

Marjorie Kyte-Hopper's
Life is Just A Lottery

Hello, Dear Readers, one can never plan what is going to happen to one. Life, with all its twists and turns is not unlike a lottery draw. Everyone holds their ticket as the balls bash against each other hoping their numbers come up. Then they is disappointment and then hope the next draw day and so it goes in a circle of hope and despair. It's very sad!

BUT NOT FOR ME!! Readers, numbers have come up, 20 MILLION QUID... Yeah! I can leave this pile of shit magazine at last and enjoy myself......sorry. Please forgive me for my out of place outburst. Let's all hope that one day YOUR numbers will come up, until then, persevere, hope and wish.

I have asked the Commissioning Editors to remove my picture and by-line as I no longer wish to been seen as a part of this scurrilous load of old elephant dung. *Yours Aunt Marjorie*

<<<<<<<<<>>>>>>>>

Congratulatory Message

We would like to pass on our congratulations to Auntie Marjorie. We would like to wish all the best with her new found millions and hope that she will do some good with them! The Editors.

<<<<<<<<<>>>>>>>>

Dorset Barrington's
Antique ~~*Dealing*~~ *Stealing*

Dorset Barrington's interest in becoming an antique dealer was inflamed by the vast amount of profit he made from selling off various priceless family heirlooms as a child. Barrington, the husband of the now penniless Lady Valkyrie Beauderriere-Barrington, makes regular appearances on 'Crimewatch' and is most famous for his popular daytime television programme 'The Three Auctioneers.' He is now residing at Her Majesty's Pleasure in HMP Grymthorpe. Dorset wasn't able to send anything out this month, but he got someone to smuggle out his Hollywood Interview. Let's have a look at it!

<<<<<<<<<>>>>>>>>

Hollywood Interviews

Each Month one of our Columnists will interview a famous Hollywood Star. This month Dorset Barrington talks by telephone to **Tony**

Crappolini, star of many Gangster Films. This interview was transcribed from a tape recording smuggled out by Dorset.

Dorset: Hello...hello?

Tony: Si, 'allo!

Voice over phone: *Oi Fatty Barrington, get off the effin' phone!*

Dorset: Sorry about all that, so your films are mainly about the Mafia... why's that?

Tony: Itsa what I know innit, you have to go with what you know right?

Voice over phone: *Alright Barrington, times up, get you fat stupid arse back in your cell.*

Dorset: I won't be too long now. (sound of someone being hit) Ah!!

Tony: Cell! are you in prison Mr Barrington, I don't like to involve myself with criminals.

Dorset: Ha! Ha! No, no, of course not...Thruster stop doing that!"

Tony: What's going on, what's he doing to you. where are you?

Dorset: Umm...I'm on...retreat, at a monastery, to have a rest in my monk's cell.

Voice over phone: *Oi, twatface, in your fecking cell now!*

Tony: Who was that?

Dorset: Er, that was... the Father Abbot... It's time to return to our cells for meditation. I'm on my way Father!

Voice over phone: *Don't you fecking father me you fat .....*

There was then the sound of someone being hit and kicked and then the line went dead.

<<<<<<<<<>>>>>>>>

Millicent 1940's Wife
War is nearly over, and the people of England are looking forward to a bright new future.

"Dwarling?" said Millicent, as she was scouring out her husband's underpants with Vim. "Would you be *awfully* cross if I invented something called the Space Shuttle?" Millicent's husband Gordon put down his mistress and looked at his wife with a patronising raise of the eyebrow.

> You haven't been having ideas again have you poppet?

> Only silly ones that would probably make us rich Dwarling.

"Now Millie-pillie-silly-dilly," he said with a kindly smile, "you simply must get these impractical ideas out of your head. I know it sounds enjoyable inventing things, but you seem to be neglecting the housework, I know for a fact that the roof hasn't been polished in days. And anyway, there is the church rebuilding to think about and weren't you going to entertain the POW's with your dance act?

"Yes I know Dwarling." said Millicent gently replacing his penis back into his trousers with a pair of sugar tongs. "I wasn't thinking of inventing a Space Shuttle *now!*" she laughed, "I plan to wait until the 1980's, after all Susan and Robert will be involved in a guerrilla war in west Africa by then so I'll have more time." Gordon sighed and, polishing his Bakelite bicycle, said, "Come on you old daft bitch, let's not have any more talk of inventions. I am beginning to think that I should have listened to my mother, she said that you were one slice short of a tin of Spam?" Millicent bowed her head,

"Yes Dwarling," she said mournfully, "but I just thought that inventing the Space Shuttle would get us out of this awful, awful financial mess.

I've thought it all through. I've got an idea for using it to put things up in space and something I might call Satellite Communication Technology." Gordon adjusted his jock-strap and stood up. His hands grasped the back of an armchair, crushing Millicent's hand-embroidered sanitary protection.

He was really bloody livid now. "We went through all this when you had that soppy idea about tiny valves that would make radios a lot smaller.

Now let's just forget all about half-baked schemes, you sit there and think about what I said, and I'll get us both a glass of Wincarnis shall I?"

Millicent smiled to herself. Gordon was a simply splendid husband, "Promise you're not *awfully* cross Dwarling." she pleaded.

<<<<<<<<>>>>>>>

Hollywood Interviews

Each Month one of our Columnists will interview a famous Hollywood Star. This month 'Witty Man' talks to: **Jerry Mander, Top British comedy film star of such films as 'Oops, Mrs. Brown;' 'Careful, Mrs. Brown' and 'I Told You So, Mrs. Brown'**

Witty Man:	So, you're a funny man, are you?
Jerry:	I like to think so, I've been...
Witty Man:	Say something funny then!
Jerry:	Well, I can't just think of something off hand...

165

Witty Man:	Exactly. That's what I tell those bastards at the Egerton Review, but do they bloody listen, do they shit, no, it's Witty Man, say something witty, bastards!
Jerry:	Well, being funny is an art... you need to learn the craft, you...
Witty Man:	Bollocks, you're either funny or you're not, look my jobs on the line here, give me something funny!
Jerry:	Well, I'm really a joke teller, people write them for me
Witty Man:	I don't want a bleeding joke, I need witticisms!
Jerry:	I'm sorry, I can't help you...Agghh, let go of me!

It all ended in a farce.

<<<<<<<<>>>>>>>

Tracy Mugton's Wedding Journal

Well, early next mumf, me and my Timothy will be married, and we can begin our life of luxury and privilege. I said to Tim that we should 'ave our 'unnymoon in Ibiza. I've been there before and it was lovely, drinking dancing, fighting an all. Tim said perhaps it would be best if we spent it at home at the Castle.

I'm beginning to fink that 'e ain't as rich as he said 'e was. I'm sure he just wants me all to 'imself and after that secret night he visited me I know why. Right little snufflin' animal 'e was.

Anyway, my troo...trus.... all my fings I need for the wedding are ready and I can sit back and look forward to an exciting life with my Tim. I always thought that I would end up married to a loser wiv no munny, but now I'm gonna live in a Castle and one day become a lady!

See yer next mumf for the wedding, you're all invited. Tata Trac

In the Potting Shed with Old Nobby
A Selection of Non-Motivational Quotes from our resident miserable old git!

"Enjoy the good times to the full because something terrible is going to happen very soon!"

<<<<<<<<>>>>>>>

Public Eye
your observations appreciated

doppelgangers

We invite you to send in examples of look-alikes. Only the most astounding resemblances will be published.

Art Scroggins, a postman, observes. That one of the customers whose letters he delivers, looks exactly like Brig. Gen. Theodore Trumpton-Hardy under whom he served as batman during the war.

children say the funniest things!

Nothing again...the little shits!

<<<<<<<<>>>>>>>

you'll never guess who I saw!

Brig. Trumpton-Hardy says.
That my local postman bears a striking resemblance to Pte. Scroggins, my old batman who left the army to join the postal service. Uncanny isn't it? He was a good man; wish we'd kept in touch!

<<<<<<<<<>>>>>>>

Letters from our Readers
The following is a selection of the boring dreary rubbish sent to us by readers of the magazine.

Howdy Editors at The Egerton Review,
Last month Norma Westfield accused Margaret Root of being a deranged old bat. I can now clear this matter up having met Ms Root. She is a wonderful woman who has a gifted way with animals and knows how to iron a Stetson.
Stet Chetson
You mean you got off with her Stet? The Editors

Dear Editors at The Egerton Review,
Will one of you please visit me?
Dorset Barrington
Very busy running a superb publication. Would love to see you but simply can't tear ourselves away from work. Sorry. The Editors

Dear Editors at The Egerton Review,
Does Kev Mugton want his head kicked in?
Ferdinand Bell-Bloute
You'd have to ask him Ferd. The Editors

Dear Editors at The Egerton Review,
Who is Crispin Banyard and why is he always asking about me?
Neville Slipton
He's one of your fans Neville. The Editors

Dear Editors at The Egerton Review,
I recently met up Stet Chetson on his ranch. If any other people who work on The Egerton Review would like to meet me, I'd be thrilled.
Margaret Root. **P.S.** I was wrong about Stet and you were right. He is a tosser, and he definitely isn't a real American. He's never even been to Disneyworld. I'm so disappointed I'd like to have him beaten up again.
You're our new best friend Margaret. The Editors.

Dear Editors at The Egerton Review,
I was intrigued to read in last month's publication that the Countess de Verucca had given the Alfa Romeo Tiara to one of your readers. As the tiara was stolen two years ago from Harrods's Wine Department the Countess is now under suspicion and will be interviewed by the police.
Lord Whisp. Director of Artifacts Recovered.com.
Excellent, she's already in a shit load of trouble with Lord Beauderriere...now this! The Editors

Dear Editors at The Egerton Review,
I'm so tired I can barely write.
Gerald Melton
Diddums. The Editors.

<<<<<<<<>>>>>>>

OBITUARIES
We do not have entries for this section this month. C'mon, do you want to live forever!!

PERSONAL
Work Wanted...Supervisory Magazine Publishing Preferred. Contact: The Fed-Up Editors

<<<<<<<<>>>>>>>

The Egerton Review

Things you never wanted to know, told to you by people who know nothing about them

Vol. 1   July 2004

Stet Chetson, ex-chairman, twat, idiot, punchbag, irrelevant dickhead. Just to look at him you want him beaten up again.

Issue bloody 7 contains er... blah, blah, blah, Dorset Barrington, blah, blah, blah, Neville Slipton and BLAH!!!! I should be on bloody holiday not stuck in this god forsaken office pandering to your whims and desires....Thank you for buying this copy.

<<<<<<<<<>>>>>>>>

Why don't you just piss off Chetson you Non-American tosser!

This article is sponsored by
The Sworn Enemies of Stet Chetson
(Chigwell Branch)

<<<<<<<<<>>>>>>>>

Darcy Copperfield's
Literature Unleashed

At the tender age of ten Darcy Copperfield was expelled from St. Peregrine's School for Boys for writing 'Anne of Green Gables is a nymphomaniac' on the blackboard. Blah, Blah Blah!!

Darcy is staying in the secure unit of the McNutters Institute as he is still extremely unwell. There will be no copy from him for quite a while. We do not believe that Darcy will ever return to the Review, the signs are not good.

The Doctor telephoned us to give us update and told us of Darcy's wild-staring eyes, dribbling, heavy breathing and what appears to be a condition called Priapism. We wanted to tell the Doctor that this was normal for Darcy but were afraid that would discharge him into our care. We don't want that!

COULD YOU WRITE EROTIC FICTION?

Send your exotic fantasies, in the form of a short story, to Darcy Copperfield c/o The Egerton Review for use in any other edition of the Review or for Darcy's personal files. Please include a photograph of yourself. Sorry we can't return submissions.

It will give him some to read in those cold grey early hours of the morning as he contemplates his mortality

<<<<<<<<>>>>>>>

Neville Slipton's
Language Workshop
"My tongue is my passport"

Neville Slipton was born Susan Grace Sliptonova in 1956. His deep interest in, and unrivalled grasp of, languages stemmed from living in a multi-lingual environment in no less than forty-three countries.
He is never happier than when he is able to use his talent with his tongue in any corner of the world.

Hi-De-Hi

I thought I would introduce 'Melty' gently to my column. We decided to take the train to the coast and try our hand at Holiday Camps. We were met at the station by the Camp Bus, we got on board with an assortment of fellow campers and set off for the camp.

We arrived and queued up at the Reception Desk, "Bonne Motte," I said, "party of two, what time is dinner?"

A rather dishevelled young lady at the desk looked up and said, "Name?." I looked at the badge pinned to her ample bosom and said, "Apparently your name is Mandy."

"Nah, not mine, yours!" she replied rather acidly. I gave her my name and she said, "Chalet 26, north side. We waited for a while, but it seemed that there was no one to help us with our valises, we made our way to Chalet 26 North side. At dinner time we entered the *'Chambre de mange'* and looked to catch the eye of the waiter. It was after a while that we discovered that it was something called 'self-service.' At the counter we saw an array of what passed for food. I asked a rather spotty young man if he had any 'pâté,' he told me that she works in the 'arcades.'

Melty and I looked at each other, and with unspoken words returned to Chalet 26 North Side, collected our luggage and left the camp for the most expensive hotel in the area. We vowed never to set foot in such a place again. Melty did tell me that he was rather reluctant to leave as he had put his name down for the 'Pertest Bottom

Competition' I told him that, in my opinion, he would have won hands down. Hey Ho!

<<<<<<<<<>>>>>>>

at home with...
The Beauderrieres

Lord Beauderriere, in his ignorance, believes that the general viewing public is chomping at the bit to hear of the exploits of this dissolute excuse for an aristocrat. To my eyes, it's just a feeble ruse to relive his salad days. He prefers to use a picture of himself in his younger days as any picture of him now would scare the horses and small children.

A SCRIPT FOR TELEVISION

EPISODE 7: LORD BEAUDERRIERE AND TRACY MUGTON

SCENE 1 (IN WHICH LORD BEAUDERRIERE IS GOGGLE-EYED AND FIRM)

CAST
LORD B - A FAT ARISTOCRAT
TRACY-LORD B'S SOON-TO-BE DAUGHTER-IN-LAW

INT: LORD BEAUDERRIERE'S BEDROOM
LORD B. IS SITTING, HIS BUTTOCKS STRAINING, IN A TATTERED WICKER CHAIR.

LORD BEAUDERRIERE:
I say, Tracy How about letting me cop a quick snog?

TRACY:
You filthy git, I'll tell yer son abart you!

LORD BEAUDERRIERE:
I'm very rich and important you snivelling commoner.
Do as I say, or I'll report you to the Egerton Review!

TRACY:
I ain't scared of no well-respected, well-written, prize winning highly prized top ten magazine!

LORD BEAUDERRIERE:
They paid you to say that didn't they?

Next Month: Lord Beauderriere And The Donkey Sanctuary

<<<<<<<<<>>>>>>>

Dr. Makitupp Azugoalong's
Quick Clinic

All too aware that medical jargon and detailed diagnoses can worry patients, Dr Azugoalong, an Iron Maiden fan, set up the first on-line East European Monosyllabic Medical Response Clinic in 1998. Dr Azugoalong speaks very little English.

Dear Doctor Azugoalong,
You may recall that I wrote to you in a while ago to tell you that I am pregnant and that you are the father. Am I right in thinking that you will be making regular maintenance payments?
No.

Dear Doctor Azugoalong

I think I've lost my sense of humour. I used to have an answer for everything. Do you think it's likely that I'll lose my job as the Egerton review in house witster?
Yes

Dear Doctor Azugoalong

I am a well-known literary critic who sees sexual innuendo in everything I read. Now I am finding the text of the phone book sexy. Is there a cure?
No

Dear Doctor Azugoalong

A friend of mine burst out laughing when reading your column. Should I refuse to have anything more to do with her.
Yes.

Dear Doctor Azugoalong

I keep repeating myself. I have to say everything twice, is that a sign of mental illness?
Yes

Dear Doctor Azugoalong

I keep repeating myself. I have to say everything twice, is that a sign of mental illness?
No.

<<<<<<<<>>>>>>>

'Zen' Sven's
Sphere of Enigma

Dear Old 'Zen' has gone on a retreat to Tibet (we are obviously paying him too much) to find enlightenment and Nirvana. Whether he is successful is all down to his insight, intelligence, and sharpness of wit, so, he won't achieve anything but snow blindness we expect.

<<<<<<<<>>>>>>>

Millicent 1940's Wife

War is nearly over and people throughout England are looking forward to a bright new future.

> You haven't been having ideas again have you poppet?

> Only silly ones that would probably make us rich Dwarling.

"Dwarling?" said Millicent smoothing her permanent wave efficiently. "Would you be awfully cross if I invented something called the dot.com company?"

Millicent's husband Gordon put down his newspaper and looked at his wife querulously.

"Now Millie," he said with a kindly smile, "you simply must get these daft, silly, incomprehensible ideas out of your head. I know it sounds exciting and erotic inventing things but it's hard work and you're unlikely to make any money. And anyway, there are the church flowers to poison and doesn't that boiler suit of yours need repairing?

"Yes I know Dwarling." said Millicent quickly making an origami model of the Lusitania out of an old shoebox. "I wasn't thinking of inventing a dot.com company now!" she laughed, "I plan to wait until the turn of the next century, after all Susan and Robert will be grown up by then so I'll have more time."

Gordon sighed and, polishing his Bakelite tobacco tin, said, "Come on you old silly thing you, let's not have any more talk of pie-in-the-sky inventions.

You've got to think about slaughtering that pig for supper and didn't I overhear you offering to steal old Mrs. Heaton's savings from her?"

Millicent bowed her head, "Yes Dwarling," she said mournfully, "but I just thought that inventing a dot.com company would get us out of this awful financial mess.

I've thought it all through. I have ideas that would create money like a machine without a stroke of work" Gordon adjusted his monocle and stood up.

His hands grasped the back of Millicent's head, crushing Millicent's hair bun.

He was irate now. "We went through all this when you had that silly idea about cards you carry around in your pocket instead of cash.

Now let's just forget all about hare-brained schemes, you pop up on the roof and repair the chimney stack, and I'll get on with my paper OK?" Millicent smiled to herself. Gordon was a simply marvellous husband, "Promise you're not awfully cross Dwarling." she pleaded.

<<<<<<<<>>>>>>>

Marjorie Kyte-Hopper's

Marjorie, who won millions on the lottery last month has not been in touch, so we telephoned her, and she rather abruptly told us to piss off and leave her alone. She said she did not want to be associated with our petty rag anymore and if we were to call again, she would arrange our faces. How nice!

<<<<<<<<>>>>>>>

Rick Faberge's Column
"Even things I don't like are expensive"

Rick is currently on holiday or kidnapped or chained up as a sex slave or DEAD. Who knows or cares?

So No content....No Picture

<<<<<<<<>>>>>>>

Kev Mugton's
Fine Art Course

Kev is away preparing Beauderriere Castle for the happy couple, Tracy & Timothy, when they return from their wedding. Lord Beauderriere will not recognise the place. I am beginning to think that I should have checked the holiday roster a little more closely, it seems I'm the only idiot working this month.

<<<<<<<<>>>>>>>

Dorset Barrington's
Antique ~~Dealing~~ Stealing

Dorset is now the centre of attention of his cell-mate Thruster at his bijou residence of HMP Grymthorpe in the mythical land known as 'The North.' We haven't heard from Dorset this month either. We called the prison and asked why, and we were told that Dorset is in solitary confinement for stealing blancmange from the kitchen for 'Thruster.' We assume that 'blancmange' is a prison term for some drug or other. We will have to wait.

<<<<<<<<<>>>>>>>

Tracy Mugton's Wedding Journal
A Beautiful Day And Most Of The Bridesmaids Was Had By All.

The Bride looked as you would expect Tracy Mugton to look, gaudily dressed in what could only be called a fashion atrocity.

She strode down the aisle on the arm of her father Kev. There were gasps and ooh's and ahhh's as Kev tried to walk in his new shoes that were pinching him.

They reached the altar and Kev placed Tracy's hand into the sweaty, soft palm of her soon-to-be husband.

The words were spoken, and the two walked back up the aisle to the strains of their chosen piece of music, *'Knocked them in the Old Kent Road'* and went off to the reception at the local Working Men's Club. The music was supplied by the revived 70's band '*Superstud Megastar*' without Rick Faberge, of course. The band have had to resort to weddings and Bar Mitzvah's and the like because Rick took all the money when they disbanded

Unfortunately, as it was a Working Men's Club, the ladies had to stay outside and watch the festivities through the windows. Soon to two newly-weds were off on their honeymoon, Tracy looking forward to a night of rumpty-pumpty and Timothy to a night of panic and disappointment. The rest of the group waved and smiled and then wandered home completely pissed out of their heads.

<<<<<<<<<>>>>>>>>

In the Potting Shed with Old Nobby
A Selection of Non-Motivational Quotes from our resident miserable old git

If you hate yourself remember you are not alone! I'm sure there are lots of people who hate you too!"

<<<<<<<<<>>>>>>>>

Ye olde advertisement for your delectation
The Most Sovereign Contraption Introduced to Alleviate The Discomfort of Piles

Arthur Maudsleydale's Pile Ointment Adaptor
A Discreet and Portable Pile Ointment Adaptor that can be used Anywhere without Embarrassment. Sturdy British Made Instrument using all the Latest technology that the Industry can Muster. Made of Electro-plated nickel silver.
This item also includes a Swivel Mirror for even better accuracy.

Letters from our Readers

The following is a selection of the boring dreary rubbish sent to us by readers of the magazine.

Dear Editors at The Egerton Review
Is it true that a National tabloid has paid Ed 'Thruster' Bloggs, my cell-mate, an obscene amount of money to sell some cock and bull story about me being his 'bitch' in prison
Dorset Barrington
No, it's a lie. The sum of money isn't obscene, it's a mere £20,000. The Editors

Dear Editors at The Egerton Review
In a previous issue, you stated that I had tried to seduce Charmaine, the wife of Kev Mugton. Your allegations are untrue and have been very damaging. My boyfriend has left me and Mrs. Mugton has bombarded my with telephone calls of a rather sexual nature. I am going to sue you.
Ferdinand Bell-Bloute
Best of luck then Ferdy! The Editors.
PS Sorry about the boyfriend thing and any trouble caused. It was just meant to be a jest and to massively increase circulation.

Dear Editors at The Egerton Review
Please tell Neville Slipton that Gerald Melton is a serial killer. I know this for sure as I am one of the people he murdered. I speak from the grave!!
Crispin Banyard
PS By the way, I am now utterly convinced that Neville Slipton is gay, it's that little something about him.
Rest assured that we shall pass on your rather eerie and spectral message to Neville about Gerald. We are unable to make any comment on Neville's sexuality as that would be unethical. The Editors

Dear Editors at The Egerton Review
I'm so, so tired. I feel like murdering someone!
Gerald Melton
Oh, dear Gerald, sorry to hear that. Eh... have you ever met our ex-chairman, Stet Chetson?

Howdy Editors at The Egerton Review
Margaret Root is a fickle bitch. Five minutes after finishing with me, she started visiting Digby 'Bloody' Barrington in prison. She can't be doing it for money, as Digby hasn't got any and it can be for sex as 'Thruster' Bloggs, I find from the tabloids, is very possessive. She must be a total head-case.
Stet Chetson
You're getting on our nerves Stet, however, if you have any more juicy comments about Digby let us know so we can cash in. The Editors.

Dear Editors at The Egerton Review
Ay jou iditor, pass this massage on to that stick of dip Mister of Artefax Factoria. That tiara was all mine to give away so why doncha piss off fat man. Remember I know lotsa tings bout jou.
Countess de Verucca
Can't say fairer than that! The Editors

Howdy Editors at The Egerton Review
Can anyone tell me why Margaret Root is saying such horrible things about me?
Stet Chetson
It's because you lied to her about a number of things. You lied about being an American, you lied about how good in bed you were and, most heinous of all, you told her that that pile of crap you call a country & western album was worth a listen to. The Editors.

<<<<<<<<>>>>>>>

Classified Advertisements
There has been a drop off in classified advertisements, personal and obituaries and we are seriously contemplating making some adverts up to make us look as if we are successful.
It is imperative for our well-being and bank balance that you send in advertisements, or we will be forced to close.

<<<<<<<<>>>>>>>

The Egerton Review

Things you never wanted to know, told to you by people who know nothing about them

Vol. 1   August 2004

Stet Chetson, ex-chairman, degenerate and ranchless fool

I have nothing but contempt for this excuse of a man! I mean look at him! It's the sort of face you would hire 'toughs' to smash in isn't it!, Not that we'd do anything as heinous as that...but I mean, just look at that face!

Well, Darcy is still unwell, Auntie Marjorie has won the lottery and pissed off and we are seriously thinking of following her out of the door. Neville or Gerald have supplied some copy, but we have had no other contact.

It all seemed so easy at the beginning until the rot started setting in, late copy, non-appearance of columnists. I don't know, I think I'll have a breakdown!

<<<<<<<<<>>>>>>>>

Darcy Copperfield's
Literature Unleashed

NOTHING! BLOODY NOTHING!!
It's not even worth putting his photo up!

COULD YOU WRITE EROTIC FICTION?
Send your exotic fantasies, in the form of a short story, to Darcy Copperfield c/o The Egerton Review for use in any other edition of the Review or for Darcy's personal files. Please include a photograph of yourself. Sorry we can't return submissions.

I mean someone should, this is all supposed to be a magazine not a book about 'Who's Where'

<<<<<<<<<>>>>>>>>

Neville Slipton's
Language Workshop
"My tongue is my passport"

Neville Slipton was born Susan Grace Sliptonova in 1956. His deep interest in, and unrivalled grasp of, languages stemmed from living in a multi-lingual environment in no less than forty-three countries.

Dealing with Street Traders

It was only a little while ago that I was in Marrakesh, sauntering through the *souk*, idly swinging my gentleman's handbag, my beige Pringle jumper casually cast about my shoulders. A cooling breeze finding its way up the leg of my *pantalon de toile lâches*. Melty was having a lie down in the cool of the hotel bedroom, he is complaining of being exhausted. During my walk, I espied a couple of holiday-makers of obscure origin being bothered by a group of beggar children. I walked up to the couple and swatted away the children as one would flies. The woman said to me in a voice that could crack walnuts that she thought I was very kind in helping them, and that her husband Elmer, was likewise thankful.

I walked off throwing a smile over my shoulder. About ten minutes later I was also accosted by a beggar. This one was not a child, but a man. He pulled me by my sleeve into a small alleyway. He asked me if I was interested in what he had under his robe. I said, coyly, that I might be. He produced, rather disappointedly, a selection of postcards, not the sort you would send to a maiden aunt.

Disgusted, I drew away and continued my *promenade*. I have included some helpful phrases should you be bothered by street beggars. Remember, not all beggars are after your money. My motto, divide decide and plunder *Viola*.

In English: *"Kindly remove yourself from my immediate presence as I have no intention of supplying you with shiny buttons, glittering jewellery or coinage of the realm. I understand you are starving to death, but I do not consider it my responsibility to supplement your meagre income. May I suggest that you earn some crusts by selling, perhaps, a member of your family or your PlayStation. Farewell large-eyed emaciated imp of misfortune."*

In French: *Nous vous saurions gré s'enlever de mon présence immédiate car je n'ai aucune intention de vous fournir les boutons brillants, les bijoux de scintillement ou l'invention du royaume. Je comprends que vous êtes affame à la mort mais je ne la considère pas ma responsabilité de compléter votre revenu pauvre. Peux je vous suggérer gagne quelques croûtes par la vente, peut-être, d'un membre de votre famille ou de votre PlayStation. L'adieu grand-a observé le lutin émacié du malheur.*

In Italian: *Rimuovasi gentilmente dalla mia presenza immediata poichè non ho intenzione de fornivi I tasti lucidi, i gioielli brillanti o l'invenzione del regno. Capisco che siete affamiti alla morte man on la considero la mia responsabilità di completare il vostro reddito magro. Posso suggerirlo guadagno alcune croste vendendo, forse, da un* *membro della vostre famiglia o del vostro PlayStation. L'addio gran-eyes imp emaciated di misfortunatta.*

In German: *Entfernen Sie sich bitte von meiner sofortigen Anwesenheit, da Iich keine Absicht des Lieferns Sie mit gläzenden Tasten, funkelnden Juwelen oder Prägung des Reichs habe. Ich verstehe, daß Sie zum Tod verhungernd sind, aber ich ihn nicht für meine Verantwortlichkeit, Ihr mageres Einkommen zu ergänzen halte. Mag ich Sie vorschlagen erwerbe einige Krusten durch das Verkaufen, möglicherweise, ein Mitglied Ihrur Familie oder Ihres PlayStation. Abschied groß-musterte abgezehrten kobold das Unglückes.*

<<<<<<<<>>>>>>>

at home with...
The Beauderrieres

Lord Beauderriere, in his ignorance, believes that the general viewing public is chomping at the bit to hear of the exploits of this dissolute excuse for an aristocrat. To my eyes, it's just a feeble ruse to relive his salad days.

A SCRIPT FOR TELEVISION

EPISODE 8: LORD BEAUDERRIERE AND THE DONKEY SANCTUARY

SCENE 1 (IN WHICH LORD BEAUDERRIERE IS STRANGELY REMINISCENT AND FIRM)

CAST

LORD B - A FAT ARISTOCRAT
BLOSSOM - A DONKEY

INT: LORD BEAUDERRIERE'S EXTENSIVE GROUNDS

LORD B. IS SITTING, HIS BUTTOCKS STRAINING, IN A TATTERED WICKER CHAIR.

LORD BEAUDERRIERE:
I say Blossom, what would you do for a carrot?

BLOSSOM:
Hee Haw!

LORD BEAUDERRIERE:
I'm very rich and important you snivelling excuse for a horse. Nibble on this or I'll report you to Blackpool Pleasure Beach!

BLOSSOM:
Hee Haw! Hee Haw!

LORD BEAUDERRIERE:
I thought you'd give in, now where's that orange paint?

NEXT MONTH: LORD B AND THE BUTCHER.

<<<<<<<<>>>>>>>

The Life of a Country Estate Gamekeeper
By Oscar Mellers

"Nothing beats rising early, picking up your shotgun and stout walking stick and striding out across the estate for early morning inspection. A quick chat with his Lordship and then you're off to trap as many rabbits as you can and sell them to the local butcher before his Lordship is aware of any funny business going on, money in pocket old chum, money in pocket!"

<<<<<<<<>>>>>>>

'Zen' Sven's
Sphere of Enigma

We received a postcard from 'Zen' who is currently on retreat. No stamp and the content was just as boring and stupid as the man himself.

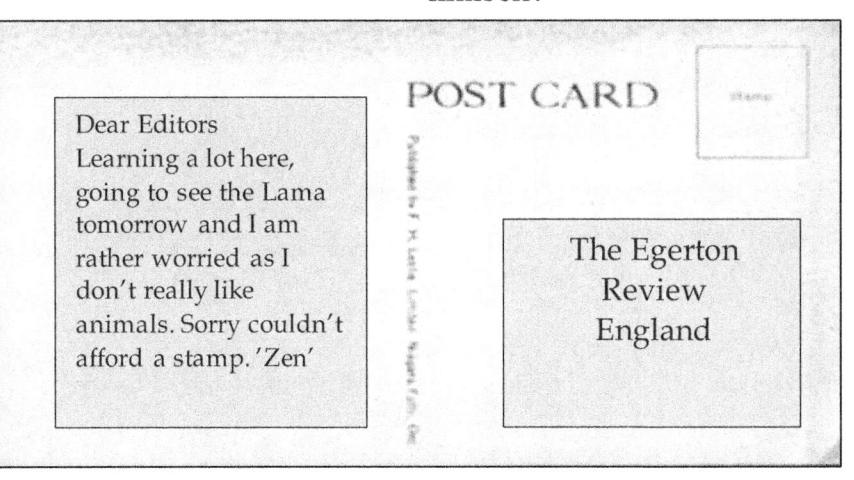

> **POST CARD**
>
> Dear Editors
> Learning a lot here, going to see the Lama tomorrow and I am rather worried as I don't really like animals. Sorry couldn't afford a stamp. 'Zen'
>
> The Egerton
> Review
> England

Text Message From History

I overheard this conversation in the Space Lunar module just before it took off for earth, "No, Neil, you did not give me the ignition key".

<<<<<<<<<>>>>>>>>

Dr. Makitupp Azugoalong's
Quick Clinic

All too aware that medical jargon and detailed diagnoses can worry patients, Dr Azugoalong, an Iron Maiden fan, set up the first on-line East European Monosyllabic Medical Response Clinic in 1998. Dr Azugoalong speaks very little English.

Dear Doctor Azugoalong,
I have been enjoying a close relationship with a fellow prison inmate. Recently, some nosy woman has been visiting my 'friend.' Since this woman, I feel that our sex life has become a shambles. I don't know what to do, I've thought of trying to kill this woman, but I can't risk spending any more time locked up as I have plans to become a 'kiss-and-tell' specialist upon my release. Do you think I should get my own back by telling the tabloids all kinds of lies about my 'friend' for money?
Yours 'Thruster'
Yes, it sounds like fun!

Dear Doctor Azugoalong
I'm not Swedish. Does that matter?
No.

Dear Doctor Azugoalong
Is there an ointment I can use to make me look younger than I am?
Yes.

Dear Doctor Azugoalong
My mother says that you are a lot older than you actually are. Is that true?
Yes.

<<<<<<<<>>>>>>>

Rick Faberge's Column
"Even things I don't like are expensive"

We have heard nothing from Rick Faberge. Nothing in the society magazines or tabloid press. We can only assume that he is still languishing on holiday somewhere and keeping a low profile...lucky bastard!

<<<<<<<<>>>>>>>

Kev Mugton's
Fine Art Course

Don't know where he is and don't care! Can't see this load of old rubbish lasting very long... we had big ideas y'know!

<<<<<<<<<>>>>>>>

Millicent 1940's Wife
War is nearly over and people throughout England are looking forward to a bright new future.

"Dwarling?" said Millicent washing herself I bath "Would you be awfully cross if I invented something called the wet room?" Millicent's husband Gordon stood up from the lavatory and wiped his arse and looked at his wife askance.

"Now Millie," he said with a kindly smile, "why do you always interrupt me when I'm on the loo, you know it puts me off.

You haven't been having ideas again have you poppet?

Only silly ones that would probably make us rich Dwarling.

Never mind crackpot inventions, why don't you invent a softer toilet paper? And anyway, orphans need to be taken to the zoo to feed the lions and the old vegetable patch needs turning back into a lawn?

"Yes I know Dwarling." said Millicent quickly dusted herself with talcum powder. "I wasn't thinking of inventing a wet room now!" she laughed, "I plan to wait another few years, after all Susan and Robert will not be under my feet then."

Gordon sighed and, polishing his Bakelite toilet roll holder, said, "Come on you old silly pookintins, let's not have any more talk of weird inventions. You've got to think about slaughtering Mrs. Heaton, and didn't I overhear you offering to give old Mr. Heaton the time of his life?"

Millicent bowed her head, "Yes Dwarling," she said mournfully, "but I just thought that inventing a wet room would get us out of this awful financial mess. I've thought it all through. No bath or shower, everything runs into a drain and...." Gordon adjusted his monocle and stood up. His hands reached out towards Millicent's breasts. He was aroused now, irate, angry, and aroused now. "We went through all this when you had that silly idea about digging a tunnel under the channel.

Now let's just forget all lunatic schemes and I'll pop and make us a lovey mug of Horlick's OK?" Millicent smiled to herself. Gordon was a simply marvellous husband, "Promise you're not awfully cross Dwarling." she pleaded.

<<<<<<<<<>>>>>>>>

Hollywood Interviews

Each Month one of our Columnists will interview a famous Hollywood Star. This month Millicent 1940's Wife talks to: **Todd Thrust, Romantic lead of such films as: 'Now Daytripper; 'Encounter in Briefs'**

Millicent: Hello Dwarling, I hope you don't mind me asking you a few little questions.

Todd: Of course not, ask away.

Millicent: You acted in some memorable films with such beautiful actresses, did you ever become romantically involved with any of them?

Todd: Of course, we were young and hot in those days! You're very beautiful. Are you married?

Millicent: Oh yes, to a Dwarling man, Gordon, we spend many an evening polishing his meerschaum.

Todd: Sounds rather boring, have you ever considered leaving him?

Millicent:	Once or twice...but not yet.
Todd:	Come away with me, I can make you happy, this husband of yours sounds a right prick.
Millicent:	I can't, not yet, Susan and Robert, my children, still need a happy loving home, perhaps later.
Todd:	Oh well, I must be going.
Millicent:	Promise you not awfully cross.

<<<<<<<<>>>>>>>

Dorset Barrington's
Antique ~~Dealing~~ Stealing

Had a garbled phone call from Dorset, worried about being 'Thrustered' or something, We just don't know!

<<<<<<<<>>>>>>>

Countess de Verucca's
Liquid Lunch

We thought we had received some communication from the Countess on our answering machine, but it was just interference and static so bollocks to her!

<<<<<<<<>>>>>>>

In the Potting Shed with Old Nobby
A Selection of Non-Motivational Quotes from our resident miserable old git!

"Remember you've only got one body and...bloody hell, you ruined it already!"

<<<<<<<<>>>>>>>

Letters from our Readers
The following is a selection of the boring dreary rubbish sent to us by readers of the magazine

Dear Editors. at The Egerton Review,
I love Millicent's column in your magazine but wonder if she really thinks that her husband Gordon is such a super chap? He seems a bit of a chauvinist to me.
Ms. G Richards
We're with you Ms. Richards, he does seem a bit of a tosser doesn't he? The Editors.

Dear Editors. at The Egerton Review,
Is Marjorie Kyte-Hopper a man? She seems to have rather broad shoulders and a certain butchness. I'm intrigued.
Diana (David) Smedley *Croydon Transvestite Club*
As far as we're concerned Auntie Marj is all woman. Her burly appearance can be put down to her country upbringing and her regular testosterone injection. The Editors.

Dear Editors. at The Egerton Review,
I love Millicent's column in your magazine but wonder if she really thinks that her husband Gordon is such a super chap? He seems a bit of a chauvinist to me. Yours,
Ms. G Richards
We're with you Ms. Richards, he does seem a bit of a tosser doesn't he? The Editors.

Dear Editors. at The Egerton Review,
I had to write to let you know that one of my erotic stories was selected by Darcy Copperfield as a prize winner. Darcy Copperfield, who wrote to tell me he thoroughly enjoyed 'Oily Swedish Au Pair Eats A Banana' also invited me to tea at his penthouse apartment in Bloomsbury Square. I'm so happy I might even consider going to bed with him.
Ingrid Boobssen PS I'm not Swedish, will that matter?
Probably not. The Editors.

Dear Editors. at The Egerton Review,
I've written to your magazine on numerous occasions, but you never print my letters. Instead, you seem intent on publishing ongoing written communications between certain members of your staff and the general public. I'd dearly love to have a letter printed in your magazine but fear that I don't write about the kind of things that would interest very high brow people like yourselves. Have you any advice for me?
Millie Wharmley
It's very difficult to define what exactly makes a letter worth publishing. The one you sent recently is a very good example of a very boring letter. Hence it isn't the sort of thing we would consider for publication. The Editors.

Dear Editors. at The Egerton Review,
Ignore my warning about Gerald Melton at your peril.
Crispin Banyard
Note: It is the policy of The Egerton Review not to respond to communication from the dead. Therefore, Crispin Banyard's letters will be unanswered and shredded after publication. The Editors.

<<<<<<<<<>>>>>>>>

ENDORSEMENT:
"We've never heard of the Egerton Review,
now go away before I call the police."
Results of Street Brawl
(conducted in Clacton)

The Egerton Review

Things you never wanted to know, told to you by people who know nothing about them

Vol. 1 September 2004

Stet Chetson... 'Nuff Said!!

Well, September is here, and we seem to be getting to the bottom of available copy to show you. We have scouring the archives and have found some interesting things. We haven't heard from Neville or the Countess or any of them really, so we have decided to give you what we have and hope for the best. We honestly can't see the Review lasting much longer.

<<<<<<<<<>>>>>>>>

Darcy Copperfield's
Literary Unleashed

At the tender age of ten Darcy Copperfield was expelled from St. Peregrine's School for Boys for writing 'Anne of Green Gables is a nymphomaniac' on the blackboard. Waffle, waffle, waffle, probably all lies anyway!!!

Darcy has come out of his coma to send us this copy, reading it, and letting Auntie Marjorie edit was a waste of time and energy, but it fills a page so hey ho! *"I have received this witty and informative little story from a charming young woman who went down on her knees to beg me to put this in this month's issue. So, I have, read on and enjoy!"*

Oily Swedish Au Pair Eats A Banana
by Ingrid Boobssen
(she's not Swedish but that doesn't matter.)

This story has been previously edited by Marjorie Kyte-Hopper our 'what is decent' advisor and resident prude.

As I am not Swedish, I have always thought I would be useless in bed. But then I met xxxxxxxxxxxxxxxx who taught me a thing or two about xxxxxxxxxxxxxxxx and xxxxxxxxxxxxxxxx.

Naturally, I was amazed that a banana could be used to xxxxxxxxxxxxxxxx and xxxxxxxx, not only that, that it was still edible afterwards. At first, I was nervous about xxxxxxxx and nearly gagged when xxxxxxxxxxxxxxxx put the xxxxxxxx into my, but the oil ensured that there was no xxxxxxxxxxxxxxxx.

I was so xxxxxxxxxxxxxxxx that I screamed and soon we did it again. I decided that xxxxxxxxxxxxxxxx was a really good position. Xxxxxxxxxxxxxxxx would be the xxxxxxxxxxxxxxxx which is favoured by most because of the easy xxxxxxxxxxxxxxxx. I took xxxxxxxx's xxxxxxxx in my hand and gave it a firm xxxxxxxx and he began to go crazy and then toyed with my xxxxxxxx claxon. Whoooo. xxxxxxxx's nearly exploded with lust when he heard my cry of delight. Then he increased the pressure of the xxxxxxxx, !!! Agggghhhhhhh. We were both completely satisfied.

I had never heard of Arthur Maudsleydale before, but I'm glad I have now. My xxxxxxxx have got much bigger. And so have my bosoms.

(We hope the story kept you glued to your seat despite the omissions)

<<<<<<<<>>>>>>>

Neville Slipton's
Language Workshop
"My tongue is my passport"

We still haven't heard from Neville; Gerald tells us that Neville is rather under the weather . He said he is taking Neville for a caravan holiday and hopes that Neville will be back to normal before the Christmas Issue. We are not sure what sort of 'normal' he means

at home with ....
The Beauderrieres

Lord Beauderriere, in his ignorance, believes that the general viewing public is chomping at the bit to hear of the exploits of this dissolute excuse for an aristocrat. To my eyes, it's just a feeble ruse to relive his salad days.

A SCRIPT FOR TELEVISION

EPISODE 9: LORD BEAUDERRIERE AND THE BUTCHER

SCENE 1 (IN WHICH LORD BEAUDERRIERE IS FIRM AND FIRM)

CAST:

LORD B - A FAT ARISTOCRAT
FILLETT - LORD B'S BUTCHER

INT: LORD BEAUDERRIERE'S KITCHEN
LORD B. IS SITTING, HIS BUTTOCKS STRAINING, IN A TATTERED WICKER CHAIR.

LORD BEAUDERRIERE:
I say Filletty, I bet you'd like this on your block?

FILLETT:
I don't deal in scrag end!

LORD BEAUDERRIERE:
I'm very rich and important you snivelling tradesman
Bone and roll this or I'll report you to Smithfield Meat Market!

FILLETT:
Put it away or I'll get my chopper out!

LORD BEAUDERRIERE:
Really? That's all I ask.

NEXT MONTH: LORD BEAUDERRIERE AND THE HALLOWEEN PARTY

<<<<<<<<<>>>>>>>>

It seems to me the Lord Beauderriere is the only constant contributor to this esteemed magazine. The fact that the content of his contribution is rather below the belt at time it is obvious that he had been pounding away relentlessly so to enhance the prestige of this publication. Noblesse Oblige indeed!

<<<<<<<<<>>>>>>>>

The Life of a Country Estate Gamekeeper
By Oscar Mellers

"Nothing beats rising early, picking up your shotgun and stout walking stick and striding out across the estate for early morning inspection.
A quick chat with his Lordship and then you're of to suck out as much trout from the river using my patented 'Mellers Trout Sucking Unit' and sell them to the local fishmongers and restaurants you can before his Lordship is aware of any funny business going on, money in pocket old chum, money in pocket!"

<<<<<<<<<>>>>>>>>

Countess de Verucca's
Liquid Lunch

? ? ? ? ? ? ? ? ? ?

We currently have no idea where The Doctor, Rick, Kev, Marjorie or Dorset are, and we don't give a flying fart. It will all be over soon!!

<<<<<<<<<>>>>>>>

Oh, wait! We do have a Marjorie Hollywood Interview on file and here it is.

<<<<<<<<<>>>>>>>

Hollywood Interviews

Each Month one of our Columnists will interview a famous Hollywood Star. This month Marjorie Kyte-Hopper talks to Georgiana Strummer, star of many Lesbian Erotic Films such as 'Strummin,' 'Strappadictomy,' and a 'Finger of Fudge'

Marjorie: I must say that it is a pleasure to meet you.

Georgiana: I've been looking forward to this interview, I've heard so much about you.

Marjorie: Now my dear, you've made many films, and they are all about Lesbians, don't you think you've been stuck in something of a groove?

Georgiana: Yes, all my films involved Lesbians, it's my speciality, my forte, my weakness. I am, in fact, a Lesbian. Does that surprise you?

Marjorie: Oh no my dear, we all have to come from somewhere. I was born in Norfolk; you were born in Lesbia!

Georgiana: Sorry, what do you mean?

Marjorie:	The place you were born, Lesbia, you said you were a Lesbian!
Georgiana:	It's not a place Marj, it's a state of mind. It's a melding, sweetie, of like-minded people, people of the female sex.
Marjorie:	A sort of club, a club for ladies only. Like the W.I. Eh?
Georgiana:	That's right, no men allowed!
Marjorie:	What sort of things go on at your club?
Georgiana:	Allsorts. The main occupation is to help each other reach their....!
Marjorie:	Potential?
Georgiana:	That's one way of putting it. But the main event is deep and dirty sex, writhing sweaty bodies, entwined in ecstasy, each achieving a marvellous orgasm!!
Marjorie:	I see.... So, it's really just like my boarding school but without the lessons. What night of the week is it......

<<<<<<<<<>>>>>>>

Text Message From History
Poor old King John not only did the Barons force him to sign the Magna Carta, but they also got him to buy a three-year warranty as well!

Text Message From History
Her Majesty said, "I can accept the potato, Sir Walter and at a push the tobacco, but what are we going to do with the bicycle?"

Millicent 1940's Wife

War is over and the people of England are looking forward to a bright new future

"Dwarling, I completely understand that you are the head of the house and I'm just a woman, but why do you deride my inventions that I am sure will settle this financial mess we are in."

"Millicent darling, sweetie-love, I have always believed that it is the man of the house's job to provide an adequate income and that you just have to look pretty and make sure my meals are on the table when I want them."

Millicent walked over and stood behind his chair and ruffled his hair. "I see Gordon, then why are you out of work spending most of your days with your Bakelite collection?" Gordon slowly got up and faced her and said. "What do you mean by that Millicent? I am a qualified Hansom Cab driver, and jobs like them are few and far between!"

Millicent smiled, "Then why don't you get up off your bloody backside and look for a job that has NOT been obsolete for over 50 years!" Gordon stumbled back at this outburst.

"This is so unlike you, you always seemed content with everything, we have a little money coming in each week, we get by!"

"We have a little money coming in Gordon because I spend my nights up at the US Air Base giving blow-jobs to flyers for 2/6d a time!!"

"Blow-job, what's that?" enquired Gordon. "If you've got half a crown, I'll show you!" shouted Millicent.

Gordon took out his Bakelite purse and looked in it. "I don't suppose you could lend me sixpence sweetypoos!" At that moment something in Millicent snapped and she calmly walked to the coal cellar, picked up the coal-hammer and returned to the lounge, Gordon was standing at the window contemplating which of his Bakelite artifacts he could pawn for 2/6 when the coal-hammer came crashing down on his skull.

He dropped to the floor quite dead, and Millicent knelt down beside his lifeless body.

Millicent spent the rest of the day building a Hand-Hade Time Machine from all the bits and bobs she had been working with during the year.

She dragged the Hand-Made Time Machine into the lounge and looked down at the lifeless Gordon.

Gordon was a simply splendidly dead husband, "Promise you're not *awfully* cross Dwarling." she pleaded. She turned the dial of the Hand-Made Time Machine to the early 21st century and pushed the lever and disappeared in a cloud of smoke.

Well, that was a surprise, I wonder if we will hear from Millicent again!!

I must I'm a bit surprised that it took nearly a year for Millicent to rid herself of that Bakelite anchor of a husband. We can only hope that the future will look better for her and the kids!

<<<<<<<<>>>>>>>

In the Potting Shed with Old Nobby
A Selection of Non-Motivational Quotes from our resident miserable old git!

"When someone says to you, 'everything happens for a reason,' kick them in the bollocks and say 'That was meant to be'

<<<<<<<<>>>>>>>

Letters from our Readers

The following is a selection of the boring dreary rubbish sent to us by readers of the magazine.

Dear Editors. at The Egerton Review,
I want to marry Margaret Root but can't seem to shake Ed 'Thruster' Bloggs off. He's started threatening me.
Dorset Barrington
Is Thruster Swedish by any chance? The Editors.

Dear Editors. at The Egerton Review,
I'm suspicious about 'Zen' Sven. As there is never a picture of him, I don't think he actually exists.
Mary Donizetti
He does exist Mary. Think of it this way, we don't have a picture of you but that doesn't mean we immediately jump to the conclusion that you're imaginary. The Editors.

Dear Editors. at The Egerton Review,
I nearly strangled Neville Slipton with a chiffon scarf the other night. I seem to be going psychotic.
Gerald Melton
It doesn't surprise us. The Editors.

Dear Editors. at The Egerton Review,
I had to write again to let you know that one of my erotic stories was selected by Darcy Copperfield as a prize-winner. Darcy Copperfield, who wrote to tell me he thoroughly enjoyed 'Oily Swedish Au Pair Eats A Banana' also invited me to tea at his penthouse apartment in Bloomsbury Square. I'm so happy I might even consider going to bed with him.
Ingrid Boobssen P.S. I'm not Swedish, will that matter?
Bugger off, you wrote to us last month Ingrid. This is publicity seeking of an extreme nature. The Editors.

Dear Editors. at The Egerton Review
I've written to your magazine numerous times, but you never print any of my letters. Instead, you seem intent on publishing ongoing written communications between certain members of your staff and the general

public. I'd dearly love to have a letter published in your magazine but fear that I don't write the kind of thing that would interest highbrow people like yourselves. Have you any advice for me yet?
Millie Wharmley
For heaven's sake, you're as bad as Ingrid Boobssen (see above). Go away. Nobody would enjoy your poxy letters anyway. You're wasting our time. The Editors.

Dear Editors. at The Egerton Review
Please inform the Police about Gerald Melton. You are all in grave danger.
Crispin Banyard
Note: It is still the policy of The Egerton Review not to respond to communications from the dead. Therefore, Crispin Banyard's letter will be unanswered and shredded after publication. The Editors.

<<<<<<<<>>>>>>>

The Egerton Review

Things you never wanted to know, told to you by people who know nothing about them

Vol. 1   October 2004

Stet Chetson, our ex-chairman with the help of a neighbour has managed to lost most of his ugly fat

Stet Chetson now decapitated (see Letters Page) is probably not in a position to sell his ranch. This is probably a good thing as we have found out that he hasn't got a ranch.

I am sure all our readers will join in with us when we say bloody good job to whoever did this marvellous piece of reconstructive surgery on our ex-Chairman.

The Egerton Review is looking for a new chairman to assist us financially in running this magazine. We are looking for someone with the following attributes:
1. A head.
2. Money
3. No idea about publishing a magazine

These are a prerequisite for the post as we don't want any interference in our work.

<<<<<<<<<>>>>>>>>

Darcy Copperfield's
Literature Unleashed

The following three months will contain just snippets of copy as the columnists have disappeared and we don't really care where they are. We hope it doesn't spoil your enjoyment of the magazine.

Once again Darcy has lapsed into a coma and this time, I think we will just leave him in the helping, healing hands of the medical profession. As we have a morbid feeling that a vacancy will soon arise in the Literary Department......

<<<<<<<<<>>>>>>>>

At home with ....
The Beauderrieres

Lord Beauderriere, in his ignorance, believes that the general viewing public is chomping at the bit to hear of the exploits of this dissolute excuse for an aristocrat. To my eyes, it's just a feeble ruse to relive his salad days.

A SCRIPT FOR TELEVISION

EPISODE 10: LORD BEAUDERRIERE AND THE HALLOWEEN PARTY

SCENE 1 (IN WHICH LORD BEAUDERRIERE IS FIRM AND TUMESCENT)

CAST

LORD B - A FAT ARISTOCRAT
MASKED GUEST - A MASKED GUEST

INT: LORD BEAUDERRIERE'S BALLROOM
LORD B. IS SITTING, HIS BUTTOCKS STRAINING, IN A TATTERED WICKER CHAIR.

LORD BEAUDERRIERE:
I say you, what do you want, trick, or treat?

MASKED GUEST:
I'm only here for the vol-eu-vents!

LORD BEAUDERRIERE:
I'm very rich and important you snivelling mystery person
Pull my party popper or I'll report you to the Witch of Endor

MASKED GUEST:
Is that a trick or treat?

LORD BEAUDERRIERE:
Let's find out!

NEXT MONTH: LORD BEAUDERRIERE AND BONFIRE NIGHT

<<<<<<<<<>>>>>>>>

In the Potting Shed with Old Nobby
A Selection of Non-Motivational Quotes from our resident miserable old git!

"The best things in life are NOT free, they are bloody expensive

<<<<<<<<>>>>>>>

Letters from our Readers
The following is a selection of the boring dreary rubbish sent to us by readers of the magazine.

Dear Editors at The Egerton Review
I'm so pleased that Millicent finally realised what a jerk Gordon was. I read about his murder with glee and relief.
Ms. G Richards
It was great, wasn't it. The Editors

Dear Editors at The Egerton Review
My name is Millicent, and I have travelled here in a Hand Made Time Machine. My question is, can I be charged for murder if the murder took place in the 1940's.
Mrs. Millicent Buxton (1940's Widow)
You could still be arrested and charged for the crime if you were actually a real person, but as you are a fictional character, we think you will get with it. Also, there is the fact that your husband was a stereotype, and this alone would probably justify his murder. The Editors.

Dear Editors at The Egerton Review
Diana (Davis) Smedley, who jokingly suggested I was a man sounds like a person with a wonderful sense of humour. Where would we be without cheery chaps like him?

Just for the record Mr. Smedley, I'm not a man but my, thus far, dormant lesbian tendencies are rushing to the forever since a lovely lady by the name of Millicent crash-landed her Hand Made Time Machine in my vegetable patch. Isn't life full of twists and turns.
Marjorie Kyte-Hopper
It certainly is Marjorie. The Editors.

Dear Editors at The Egerton Review
I won't be writing my column this month as I have a very sore throat.
Neville Slipton
Get Gerald to wrap a chiffon scarf around your neck Neville and go to bed. The Editors

Dear Editors at The Egerton Review
I really enjoyed Ingrid Boobssen's story of the Banana. I've worked for a banana supplier for many years now, but since reading her imaginative tale I have been looking at my job in a new light and with renewed vigour.
Marcus Gellerhoop
PS I am from Swindon, does that matter?
No, it's only if you're from Sweden or not from Sweden that you need to mention your nationality or habitat. You've obviously missed the point. Too surreal for you perhaps Marcus. The Editors.

Dear Editors at The Egerton Review
I am writing to tell you how much I enjoyed Millie Wharmley's letter (Sept Letter Page) and urge you to make her a columnist. Her observations were so interesting, and she writes with such style I can't believe some like Miss. Wharmley has not written a book or won a literary prize. The world is mad, isn't it?
Gretchen Jensen PS I am Swedish
Lots of people are Swedish Gretchen, it's not really relevant. Sorry. We won't be publishing anymore of Millie Wharmley's letter. The Editors.

Dear Editors at The Egerton Review
Why won't you print anymore of my letters? Is it because I'm not from Sweden or Swindon?
Millie Wharmley

Dear Editors. at The Egerton Review
I go absolutely raving mad when reading your magazine and it reached a point last month when I decapitated my next-door neighbour because I got over excited.

I then threw the head at a passing Hand-made Time Machine that had suddenly materialised above me causing to crash-land in a Norfolk vegetable patch. My next door neighbour was an American I believe, does that matter?
Name and Address withheld.
So glad you are enjoying The Egerton Review. It doesn't really matter what nationality a person is once they have been decapitated. The Editors.

NOTE: Please do not decapitate your neighbours after reading our magazine as it puts us in a bad light.

<<<<<<<<<>>>>>>>>

The Egerton Review

Things you never wanted to know, told to you by people who know nothing about them

Vol. 1   November 2004

Stet Chetson, our recently decapitated ex-chairman

Well, we've managed to get to November and might, just might reach our Christmas Issue. Anyway, Millicent is now living with Marjorie and they both seem very happy, perhaps a little good has come out of this monumental load of old bollocks. Rick has sent us his Hollywood Interview and a letter, so he's still alive.

So, it's November, but don't expect a goodly dollop of Guy Fawkes references and the odd mention of the Houses of Parliament being blown up (or not being blown up). We're not in the mood. Speaking of things being blown up, you now have the chance to blow up (as in inflate) our columnists.

The well-known (what do you mean you've never heard of it) company INFLATAMATE will produce lifelike PVC replicas of our staff for your enjoyment.

We think this means that our publication has finally soared to the heights we once dreamed it would. (See Advertising Box in this month's issue.)

<<<<<<<<<>>>>>>>

at home with...
The Beauderrieres

Lord Beauderriere, in his ignorance, believes that the general viewing public is chomping at the bit to hear of the exploits of this dissolute excuse for an aristocrat. To my eyes, it's just a feeble ruse to relive his salad days. He prefers to use a picture of himself in his younger days as any picture of him now would scare the horses and small children.

A SCRIPT FOR TELEVISION

EPISODE 11: LORD BEAUDERRIERE AND BONFIRE NIGHT

SCENE 1 (IN WHICH LORD BEAUDERRIERE IS SPARKLING AND FIRM)

CAST: LORD B - A FAT ARISTOCRAT
GUY FAWKES EFFIGY- AN EFFIGY!
INT: LORD BEAUDERRIERE'S GARDEN

LORD B. IS SITTING, HIS BUTTOCKS STRAINING, IN A TATTERED WICKER CHAIR.

LORD BEAUDERRIERE:
I say Fawksy, how'd like a banger in your trousers?

GUY FAWKES EFFIGY:
??????????????

LORD BEAUDERRIERE:
I'm very rich and important you snivelling bag o' straw
Light my fire or I'll report you to Punch and Judy!

GUY FAWKES EFFIGY:
??????????????

LORD BEAUDERRIERE:
I shall light your blue touch paper
And we'll retire immediately!!

NEXT MONTH: LORD BEAUDERRIERE AND SANTA CLAUS

<<<<<<<<<>>>>>>>

The Beauderriere/de Verucca Kerfuffle

Following from previous correspondence regarding this tedious and somewhat unnecessary debacle between Lord Beauderriere and the Countess de Verucca we at the office have ~~intercepted~~ come across some more missives that were sent in support of his Lordship. They are laid out below. The first is from the owner of the restaurant frequented by the Countess and her late husband

Uccello's Ristorante Classico
Roma Italia

My dear lord Beauderriere
One of my customers is tell me that you wish to make book of la Bella Contessa de Verucca. I am a good friend of her and of Vincenzo, her late husbands who died here in my own beautiful restaurant. I have

remembered this evening so clearly, La Contessa was 'ow you say? Arse ratted.

She have a lot of thirst that night. She drink some lot of vino and talk all the time about Biology. She go crazy about the new leather chairs I have put in my restaurant.

She embarrassed the waiter Paulo; she keep pulling on his moustache. Her husband is get green with envious and him say to her "I am want to kill you now, you old slipper!" La Contessa she just laugh, she slap the face of the husband and eat her spaghetti. Vincenzo, he try not to notice her and enjoy his chickens. Next, he is making a lot of noise that disturb my other customers, he is gone blue and have fall over and make a lot of damage and fiasco.

La Contessa she go white with shock, she take of the jacket of Vincenzo and go through the pockets, next she try to do the kisses of life. I say leave me alone Contessa, take your tongue out of my mouth, and look after your husbands.

It is too late; I telephoned the paparazzi and the Vatican. We did everything that we could to save the Count and all of us felt sad because he had not paid his bill

. I have let the Contessa have the meal free of the charge because I feel sorry for her. I have not seen her since that night, and she stills owes for a bottle of Chianti she drunk.

I have in my possession the last words of Count Vincenzo de Verucca. He write them down on a napkin because he had no speech because of the chickens choking him.

I am like to show you the contents of the napkin, but I would want a lot of money first.

I often sit in my restaurant in the early hours of the morning when it is quiet and remember the Count writing on the napkin and it seems to me perhaps, he could have written a cheque as well. I looks forward to you contacting me.

Yours, Guiseppe Uccello

The next letter is perhaps once of the strangest of all and calls into question the right of the Countess to bear the title.

Dobson's Peerage International
1 Burkes Street London W1

The Countess de Verucca Monaco
Dear Madam
 I am writing following the recent publicity regarding the forthcoming biography of you by the eminent writer the Lord Beauderriere. On checking our extensive records to furnish tabloids with a potted history of you lineage, I have come across a problem that you may be able to assist me with.
 According to our records, the title Countess de Verucca ceased following the death of Victoria, Countess de Verucca in a nasty Mixmaster Food mixer accident in 1986. The Countess had no issue as the last Count was rendered impotent at the sight of his wife on their wedding night.
 I would therefore like you to forward to me details and incontestable proof of your right to the style and dignity of the aforementioned title.
 Perhaps you can also assist me as to the whereabouts of the maid of the late Countess, Mildred Shufflebottom. Miss Shufflebottom disappeared on the night of the Food mixer 'accident' with all the Countess's jewellery and designer clothes.
 This information would be gratefully received by the police forces of all the civilised world. I look forward to hearing from you in the very near future.
Yours, Clarence Fink - Senior Researcher

We have dug up an old *Hollywood Interview* in which Rick Faberge talks to Stanley Eversfield.

<<<<<<<<>>>>>>>

Hollywood Interviews

.Each Month one of our Columnists will interview a famous Hollywood Star. This month, Rick Faberge talks to; **Multi-millionaire Film Producer Stanley Eversfield.**

Rick: So, you're rich are you. How rich?

Stanley:	It's rather passé talking about money, don't you think?
Rick:	No, not if you've got stacks of it. I'm stinking rich, mega-rich. I am incredibly wealthy.
Stanley:	I've had a riding boot named after me!
Rick:	Oh yeah, I've got lots of illegitimate kids named after me, beat that!
Stanley:	My name will go down in the history of film making!
Rick:	I was a famous rock star!
Stanley:	I've never heard of you!
Rick:	I've never seen any of your films!
Stanley:	I don't want you to!
Rick:	Well, I'm not!
Stanley:	I've never heard any of your songs!
Rick:	Oh, bollocks!

We will leave them comparing the size of their willies. They left the building and climbed into their limousines and raced off down the road

<<<<<<<<>>>>>>>

In the Potting Shed with Old Nobby
A Selection of Non-Motivational Quotes from our resident miserable old git!

"There is nothing to fear but fear itself....oh and spiders, I bloody 'ate spiders!"

<<<<<<<<<>>>>>>>

Letters from our Readers
The following is a selection of the boring dreary rubbish sent to us by readers of the magazine.

Dear Editors. at The Egerton Review
My silly little wife got in a bit of a tizzy, murdered me and went running off to the future in a Hand-Made Time Machine. My new friend, Crispin Banyard, urged me to write to you. He says that my wife, Millicent, is living with a Ms. Kyte-Hopper in Norfolk. I believe that this person is employed by your publication. Now I'm not the sort who kicks up a fuss about such things, but really, it's a bit off don't you think?
Mr. Gordon Buxton (Deceased)
Don't tell us Gordon, you speak from the grave. The Editors

Dear Editors. at The Egerton Review,
Hypothetical question. If Millicent did invent a time machine what materials would she use? Given that rations would still be in place I wonder how she would go about it?
Mr. Edward Bork
We'd assume that Millicent would use part of an Anderson shelter and the odd gramophone component to construct the prototype. She is, of

course, a very resourceful woman. There was also an abundance of Bakelite during that era. The Editors.

Dear Editors. at The Egerton Review
Just got wind of the fact that that Boobssen girl is cavorting with that fool Darcy Copperfield. Bit cheesed off about that as she expressed an interest in me first.
Rick Faberge
She'll soon tire of the idiot Rick, don't worry. The Editors.

Dear Editors. at The Egerton Review
Marcus Gellerhoop, who wrote to you previously is unstable. He hasn't work at the banana company since he was locked away in the Fookes Mogton-Crank Psychiatric Centre in Birmingham in 1983.

I lost track of him after he changed his name to Dan Graves and disguised himself as a woman. Hope this clarifies matters.
Brian Cookson
Oh yes, everything is as clear as day now Brian!!! The Editors.

Dear Editors. at The Egerton Review
Last week while lurking around your offices in the hope of catching a glimpse of Rick Faberge.

I spotted a man wearing a pinafore dress and sling backs hiding behind the dustbins. He had a knife and looked a bit weird. I thought I'd better let you know.
Harry Spooter-Private Detective
Thank you very much for pointing this out Harry, but there's nothing to worry about. It was just Neville Slipton on his lunchbreak. The Editors. PS We are more interested in why you are stalking Rick Faberge!

Dear Editors. at The Egerton Review
It occurred to me that Dr. Makitupp Azugoalong, as he is monosyllabic, must be unable to pronounce his own name. His first name is a three syllable word, and his surname (poor sod) has five syllables. This must be a handicap for him.
Bob Black
If you're so concerned, perhaps you would like to swap names with him then Bob. The Editors.

It continually amazes us the amount of drivel our readers send us every month, it's almost as they are written by highly educated geniuses and not the bland excuses for human beings they are.

<<<<<<<<<>>>>>>>>
Public Eye
your observations appreciated
doppelgangers

We invite you to send in examples of look-alikes. Only the most astounding resemblances will be published.

Anthony Ibsen spotted:

Guy Fawkes at The Houses of Parliament firework display. "I was a bit worried because he was waving a sparkler and writing his name in the air."

children say the funniest things

Apparently, they don't. How we totally ignored it!

you'll never guess who I saw...

Cheryl Winters spotted:
Cyrano de Bergerac at her local Rhinoplasty Clinic. "I was amazed to see him there as I thought he'd come to terms with having a big nose. I was under the impression he had a multitude of ripostes to employ as a means of deflecting insulting comment. I was almost disappointed to think that he was considering surgery

Inflatamate Apology

Inflatamate would like to apologise because they are unable to produce the latex copies of our Columnists. They say that the Columnists are all ready to fat and large and that a caricature of them inflated would be dangerous to the public and an abomination too terrifying to comprehend. The company respectfully decline to produce these, I think the word was, atrocities

<<<<<<<<>>>>>>>

We really don't care about this feeble excuse for a magazine anymore. We're just going to ride it out until the end of the year and then sue for bankruptcy

<<<<<<<<>>>>>>>

The Egerton Review

Things you never wanted to know, told to you by people who know nothing about them

Vol. 1   December 2004

Stet Chetson, our recently decapitated ex-chairman in festive mood.

Christmas Issue

Happy Christmas. Here's the update: Dorset Barrington is still in prison. Stet Chetson has been decapitated and Millicent (of 1940's wife fame) is living with Marjorie Kyte-Hopper in the country.

Darcy Copperfield has booked into a clinic for the sexually irrepressible following Ingrid Boobssen's decision to gallivant around with Rick Faberge. Well, it was to be expected, she's not Swedish.

      Everyone here in the office will enjoy a delightful seasonal stuff up. It's not often that boa-constrictor appears on a menu, but we like to think of ourselves as slightly unconventional.

When stuffing a boa constrictor, it pays to have a very long spoon, or similar, to hand. But we won't go into that. The columnists have produced a very festive issue this month, in which I mean they have added the word Christmas to their articles.

Christmas at home with....
The Beauderrieres

Lord Beauderriere, in his ignorance, believes that the general viewing public is chomping at the bit to hear of the exploits of this dissolute excuse for an aristocrat. To my eyes, it's just a feeble ruse to relive his salad days. He prefers to use a picture of himself in his younger days as any picture of him now would scare the horses and small children.

A SCRIPT FOR TELEVISION

EPISODE 12: LORD BEAUDERRIERE AND SANTA CLAUS
SCENE 1 (IN WHICH LORD BEAUDERRIERE IS SEASONAL)

CAST

LORD B - A FAT ARISTOCRAT
SANTA CLAUS- A FESTIVE SACK CARRIER

INT: LORD BEAUDERRIERE'S SITTING ROOM
LORD B. IS SITTING, HIS BUTTOCKS STRAINING, IN A TATTERED TINSEL COVERED WICKER CHAIR.

LORD BEAUDERRIERE:
I say Santy. Want to see what I've got in my sack?

SANTA CLAUS:
Ho! Ho! Ho! Have you been a good boy this year?

LORD BEAUDERRIERE:
I'm very rich and important you snivelling mythical person
Fill my stocking or I'll report you to Rudolph the Red-Nosed Reindeer!

SANTA CLAUS:
Ho! Ho! Ho! Merry Christmas! Ha! Ha!

LORD BEAUDERRIERE:
You're rather jolly for someone who only comes once a year!

<<<<<<<<<>>>>>>>>

Public Eye
Your Christmas observations appreciated
<u>doppelgangers</u>
We invite you to send in examples of look-alikes. Only the most astounding resemblances will be published

Jeremiah Clackhorne writes.
I have never seen anyone like the man in this picture and conclude that this section together with your whole magazine is a waste of time and money. How do you sleep at night?

you'll never guess who I saw!

Mrs. Butt of St. Leonards writes.
I was flicking through the Egerton Review and noticed that the man that appears in various forms in your esteemed magazine looks very like my husband, Morris, uncanny isn't it?

children say the funniest things
You'd think they would say something funny at Christmas!!

The Beauderriere/de Verucca Kerfuffle

We are still receiving letters about this bloody Beauderriere/de Verucca thing which is annoying as we lost interest in the whole thing ages ago, but hey ho, it fills up the pages. Here we publish the last of the letters we could get our hands on and hope that it's an end to it all. The first one is from the British Ambassador to the Island of Calimari to the Countess' solicitors and the other from his Lordships supporters.

The British Embassy
Calamari

Mr Jeremiah Hanns
Hanns, Neece & Boompadasey

Dear Mr Hanns
It has come to my attention that there is some controversy over the proposed biography of the Countess de Verucca by Lord Beauderriere. His Lordship is a close, personal friend of mine and I know for a fact that anything he says is the paramount truth. I would like to compound this by quoting two entries from a diary left here by his Lordship's father when he was Ambassador.

__August 23__ The Embassy: Weather hot, no rain yet. Held another reception last night for the President of Calamari and his wife, Mrs Bastado. That damn De Verucca woman gate-crashed again. I have *informed the Embassy guards that if she tries to get in again, they have my permission to shoot her on sight. When is it going to rain?*

September 9 *The Embassy: Weather hot, still no rain. I was awoken in the early hours of this morning by the sound of breaking glass. The staff and I searched high and low for a broken window only to find that damn De Verucca woman had broken in and smashed a bottle of my exquisite Chateau Parfait de Montenegro.*

We found her on the study floor expertly lapping up the wine from amongst the broken glass. She was escorted to the roof of the Embassy and thrown off. We need rain and we need it NOW!!

I think the above goes a long way in vindicating his Lordship's writing and shows that there is a lot of truth in what he says. Lord Beauderriere is a frequent visitor to the island as he visits two of his businesses here. The Calamari Leather Works and the Pedro Valentino Saddle Soap Emporium.

Many a passer-by would see his Lordship burning the midnight oil to try to get those export orders out.

They would hear him moaning as they pass, no doubt upset at the loss of any, although some bitter-minded people swear that he was moaning with lust, they have said they have seen him laying full length on a leather Chesterfield, stroking the arms of the sofa, smoking a cigarette and whispering, "Was it alright for you?"

I know nothing of this, although I must add that I have seen him looking at my leather bound volumes of the History of Calamari with more than a wistful look in his eyes, but I am sure this is just his love of history.
Yours, Sir Herbert Titt British Ambassador to Calamari

The McNutters Psychiatric Institute
Knutt Lane Chelmsford

Lord Beauderriere
Hotel Bastado
Republic of Calamari

Dear Lord
In my vork as a psychiatrist, I am often asked ze following difficult qvestion , 'Am I mad Doctor?' Usually in answer to zis I am happy to

be able to say, jah, mein patient, you are stark staring bonkers. Simple and straight to ze point und no messing. However, life vould be very boring if ve vere all sane, or loopy to ze same degree.

Sometimes I have come across patients whose diagnosis completely eludes me. Although zis is a little tiresome, it is at ze same time challenging.

Ze most fascinating and absorbing case I ever had to vork on vas zat of a jung soldier who had suddenly slipped into a severe state of Traumatic Shock Ejaculation.

His continual erections had ze effect of depriving his brain of blood supply and hence oxygen until he was little more than a blithering imbecile incapable of speech. It was not long before he lost all logical thought patterns. When I came across him at a railway station in Berlin.

I assumed that ze man vas a 'mental' casualty of war, disturbed by ze horrific sights he had vitnessed during active service. But my prognosis Vas wrong. I only realised ze gruesome nature of ze cause of zis man's psychosis when, after seven months of futile and ineffectual therapy, he was visited by ze Countess de Verucca.

My patient reacted so severely on seeing her that I had to attempt to physically remove her from ze room. She was not willing to depart and clutched at my lederhosen with I caused a diversion so that he could escape by taking her there and then on the commode. I hope that this information is useful to you.

Yours, Dr. Freidrich von McNutter.

The following one is sent from an old Nanny of his Lordship to the Countess's solicitors.

GABRIELLE MOTHERSUBSTITUTE
Chieveley Berkshire CH3 6RD

Dear Sirs
I have heard on the old nanny grapevine that my dear boy, known to you as the Earl of Beauderriere, has been receiving nasty words from a lot of naughty people, this must stop now or no jam for tea.

How well I remember the first time I set eyes on the young Lord; I knew he was destined for great things. He would often leave the night nursery, run to my room, and get into bed with me.

Oh, what fun we would have, I would tickle him, and he would have me sent down to the dungeon for a week, he knew that his status was well above mine even at that young age.

If ever the young Lord was late for dinner, he could always be found in the stable block playing with the tackle, both the horses and his own.

I will not tolerate any further aspersions cast upon my dear boy, he looks after me very well and has given me a cottage on the estate for my retirement years and it only costs me £750 per week, oh generous boy. Yours, Gabrielle Mothersubstitute

The final letter is to the Countess herself.

REV. ARCHIBALD WEERDE
St Wayne & St Sharon Church
Beauderriere Berkshire CH3 6RD

Contessa De Verucca
La Spinetta
Santa Maria Boulevard
Monaco

Madam

I was astonished when I learnt of the acrimonious malediction you have unleashed at Lord Beauderriere regarding his imminent thesis of yourself.

Lord Beauderriere has, since early childhood, been a member of this congregation and if I could have a pound for every time, I have seen him sitting in the family pew I would have a...pound.

As a young man he was a member of the church choir and was no different from the other boys save for the leather trim on his cassock. Many an evening was spent in quiet conversation with the young lord discussing world and local affairs, drinking tea and trying on leather miniskirts.

I am sure that whatever his lordship has said about you can only be the truth, so stop whinging you drunken old bat and bask in the reflected glory.

Yours, Rev. A Weerde

I am glad that, as far as we are concerned, the whole thing is over, and we can get on with what we do best...ridicule people.
Now for a laugh...That's an order!

<<<<<<<<<>>>>>>>>

A Reality Collectively Recognised
A Collection of Old Songs Thesaurasised just to fill up one of the last ever pages in this doomed rag!

My Old Man (19th century Music Hall Song)
My old man said pursue the advance guard,
And do not dilly dally on the approach.
Off went the precursor with my quarters packed in it,
I followed on with my elderly cock linnet.
I dawdled and I lingered, and then I lingered, and I dawdled,
Misplaced me direction and don't know where to go.
Oh, you can't bank on the specials like the ancient period coppers,
When you can't find your way home.

Hello. Hello, Who's your lady friend?
Ciao, Hi, who's your female chum,
Who's the diminutive lassie by your flank.
I noticed you with a teenager or two,
Oh, oh, oh, I am flabbergasted at you.
Hi, Ciao, what's you miniature amusement,
Don't you imagine your habits you ought to restore. It wasn't the young woman I saw you with at Brighton,
So, who, who, who's your lady buddy.

My Old Man's A Dustman
My aged father's a refuse collector, he sports a dustman's bonnet, He wears 'oh! I say' slacks and he resides in housing association accommodation.

<<<<<<<<>>>>>>>

Tracy Mugton's Divorce Journal
The Aftermath

We have just heard that Tracy has filed for divorce from Timothy after just 5 months of marriage. We are surprised it lasted that long. We don't know the reasons and we don't really care.

This is the last issue that will be publishing so goodbye to all the idiots that have been involved in this utter fiasco called The Egerton Review. The last few remnants are following then it's over.

I think we were slightly out of our minds when we thought that we could make a go of magazine publishing. It's harder than you think it's going to be, especially when you have to deal with the sort of columnists we do.

Hold on to your copies of the magazine, they may be worth a fortune one day, not today obviously, but one day.

<<<<<<<<>>>>>>>

In the Potting Shed with Old Nobby
A Selection of Non-Motivational Quotes from our resident miserable old git!

"The only Christmas Spirit you should have comes in a bottle and should be at least 40% proof"

<<<<<<<<>>>>>>>

Letters from our Readers
The following is a selection of the boring dreary rubbish sent to us by readers of the magazine.

Dear Editors at The Egerton Review
I'm pretty worried about everybody at The Egerton Review. You seem unconcerned that there is a serial killer on the loose. Don't you think it's suspicious that ever since Gerald Melton came on the scene, Neville Slipton hasn't been seen out and about. According to you, Neville is still writing and submitting his column, but I suspect that the words were are reading are those of Gerald Melton as Neville, I believe has been murdered some months ago. There is also the fact that Stet Chetson was found decapitated ties in with the anonymous letter you received last month about an avid reader of the magazine who decapitated his American neighbour. There is also the prowler who wears a pinafore dress and sling back shoes to consider who was seen lurking behind the bin near your office. I am also terrified that a Boa Constrictor will get one of you. What is going on?
Harriet Spargate
We don't know what's going on Harriet, we really don't know or care. But thank you for giving us a quick precis of the year. The Editors.

Dear Editors. at The Egerton Review
As it's Christmas, I thought I would tell you all to piss off. I'm a really miserable person and I get great pleasure from being horrid to people, especially at this schmaltzy time of year.
Bertrand Pound
Thank you, and a very horrible Christmas to you Bert!! The Editors.

Dear Editors. at The Egerton Review,
Many months ago, someone called Rupert Nanesque wrote to your letters page. I've been obsessed by his name ever since. It has such a marvellous exciting ring to it. Is he a ballet dancer do you think?
Miss Porgy-Fig Tap
Sorry, we don't know anything about Mr Nanesque. He does sound rather exotic, doesn't he? The Editors.

Dear Editors. at The Egerton Review,
May I take this opp to wish every 1 @ the Eg Rev a Happy Xmas?
Signore Alfredo Abbreviato
Consider it done Alf. The Eds

Dear Editors. at The Egerton Review,
I honestly thought that your columnists were fictional until I bumped into one of them in a sex shop.
Neville Grunt
Which one was it Neville? The Editors.

I really shouldn't say; I was sworn to secrecy.
Neville Grunt
Oh, go on, tell us, we'll keep it a secret. The Editors.

No honestly, I can't say.
Neville Grunt
Pointless writing then wasn't it you pervy wind-up merchant. The Editors.

Dear Editors. at The Egerton Review
I got spotted in a sex shop the other day by one of our readers. I'd hate for it to be publically known that I frequent such establishments. What should I do?
Marjorie Kyte-Hopper

<<<<<<<<>>>>>>>

Nearly Over!

<<<<<<<<>>>>>>>

Classified Advertisements

HAVE YOU SEEN THIS MAN?

There's no point denying it, you must have seen him. He's been in every issue of The Egerton Review. He is, as you will now have realised, a master of disguise, a person so physically adaptable he practically mutates. He is a virtual transformer. A metamorphic genius who can play the roles of many complicated and different characters with consummate ease.

Are You Like This Man?
~~Gullible?~~ Could you, with the correct props and expert lighting, be *The Face of the Egerton Review Blog?*

Are you ready for the whirlwind of fame and fortune and utter Swedishness that will be bestowed upon you if you DO become our new face?

This So Very Lucky Man
whose identity is being kept secret, has earned less than a pittance from being the face of the Egerton Review. As you can see from his well-cut designer shirt and the happy and joyous expression on his face, he's been living the high life and loving it.

Make Thousands
of strange faces and you could be next person we ~~take the piss out of~~ laud as our mascot.

To apply to be the next face, if we can be actually bothered to continue, please send a photograph of yourself to The Editors.

Well, we can only apologise about the fiasco that was the 2004 Egerton Review. It all begun with high hopes and expectations and ended in a farce.

Once again, we, the Commissioning Editors we profusely apologize, pocket your money and run for the hills!

I think we can be forgiven now; I mean, it was 20 years ago!

<<<<<<<<<>>>>>>>>

Our Ending

It was 20 years ago that the Egerton Review raised its weary head and tried again. It lasted for just one year and then faded into the mists of literature, remembered by no-one and loved by...well, no-one as well.

The columnists packed their bags and walked out of the editorial office without as much as a glance back. What happened to all the columnists I hear you ask?

Yes, I did, I heard someone, anyway! We have traced many, if not all of them and have found out the following.

Stet Chetson, *to paraphrase the first sentence of Dicken's 'A Christmas Carol;' "Chetson was dead, to begin with. There is no doubt about that!.' We don't know what happened to his body, we don't care. He was a pain in the arse and losing his head to an lunatic neighbour was probably the kindest thing that ever happened to him.*

Darcy Copperfield, *Following his stint at a clinic to help cure his 'problem,' he now spends his time in a twilight home for the bewildered with just his memories and some very explicit and rather good DVD's.*

Darcy readily converted to this medium from his favourite format of video's as he did with his sexual orientation. Gone are his flowing locks, his fashionable clothes and his libido. He can be seen padding around the grounds in his cardigan and slippers looking for his lost youth.

Unfortunately, his lost youth is working in a fast food restaurant in Hastings and declined to be interviewed.

Neville Slipton, *The whereabouts of Neville Slipton is something of a mystery. Neville had not been seen since shortly after employing Gerald Melton as his personal dresser.*

Gerald, on the other hand, spends his days looking after Neville's house and waiting, he says, for his return. Gerald will happily show visitors and fans of Neville around the house but is rather reluctant to show them the cellar.

Someone managed a peek in the cellar through a crack in the door and reports seeing a large trunk in the centre of the room tied up tightly with a chiffon scarf and a strange, yet pleasant seepage of some kind. We will, of course, let you know of any developments in this matter.

Lord Beauderriere, *Lord Beauderriere sits brooding his dark, dank Castle. Dark because he cannot afford to pay the electricity bills and dank because of the constant dripping water coming through the roof. What little money he had was taken by Tracy Mugton-Short-Cummings in her divorce pay out from her limp handkerchief of a husband.*

He sits alone, his naked flabby buttocks straining in a rather rickety old wicker chair.

Countess de Verucca, *The Countess has given up drinking and has retired to a nunnery in Tuscany... of course she bloody hasn't! She is probably lying in a gutter breathing her last, we just don't know!*

'Zen' Sven, *'Zen' disappeared into a swirl of smoke just after leaving the Egerton Review office for the last time. He really had disappeared from the face of the earth. When the smoke cleared someone pointed out that 'Zen' was walking down the pavement on the other side of the street. The smoke was later identified as coming from the exhaust of Witty Man's 20 year old Mini! 'Zen' was eventually tracked down to a cosy seaside boarding house where he spends his days talking, and scratching his, bollocks*

Witty Man, *Witty Man spends the last years since the Egerton Review closed performing stand up in pubs and clubs. Failing dismally at that as he did with his witticisms, he now spends his time standing on Hyde*

Park Corner ranting and raving about how the entire world is at fault for his failings in life.

Dr. Makitupp Azugoalong, Dr. Azugoalong left the Egerton Review office and climbed into the back of a lorry headed for the Continent. He had decided to return to his native land of...of...wherever the hell he came from.

Sporadic news leaks out of his home country now and again that mentions the name Azugoalong, but this name is usually linked with the President and surely, he can't be President of wherever he lives, surely...I wonder how cheap the hotels are there and if there are beaches....mmm

Rick Faberge, Rick attempted to make a comeback with his band but instead of being welcomed he was ridiculed and ignored by the music industry. He decided to build a recording studio in his house in Southern France and makes thousands of pounds a day recording other people. This obnoxious git always lands on his feet.

Kev Mugton, Professor Sir Kev Mugton R.A. is everywhere these days. After leaving the Egerton Review, he was snapped up by a TV antiques programme to act as an expert on early 20th century shit.

His incisive insight brought his to the attention of the University of Chigwell who offered him the Chair of 20th Century Artifacts. He was knighted soon after a substantial cheque was deposited in the right quarters.

Despite all of these accolades, he still pines for a Mastermind Rose Bowl and still hopes to win one. Fat chance because as we have said before, he is as thick as two miscut planks!

Marjorie Kyte-Hopper & Millicent 1940's Wife, Both Marjorie and Millicent are happily living together on Marjorie's smallholding in Norfolk. Marjorie never thought she would find love and Millicent thought she had lost it forever after bludgeoning her husband to death 60 years previously.

She arrived in a Hand Made Time Machine to start another, better life with Auntie Marjorie. They spend their days maintain the smallholding, helping out in the community and offering advice willy-nilly. Everything is perfect and it must stay that way says Millicent; "

Marjorie is a perfectly darling friend and wife and I 'm sure she won't be very cross in me saying that, would you Dwarling?"

Marjorie smiled and Millicent quietly fingered the coal hammer in her knitting basket.

Dorset Barrington, Dorset left Prison and headed for the lights of Bradford. He bought a little house there and awaiting the arrival of his friend 'Thruster' who was due out of prison very soon. He opened a little antiques business that became 'a nice little earner' and in the backroom it was the Head Office for an International Antiques Theft Syndicate and money laundering service.

Either Dorset and Thruster will prosper or, maybe HMP Grymthorpe awaits, let's wish them luck.

Old Nobby, Well considering his age he's probably dead by now. We buried him so I must assume he was dead!

Oscar Mellers the Gamekeeper, Oscar is now the Chairman of the biggest Fish and Game suppliers in the country. We wish him well.

And what about us, the two unfortunate Commissioning Editors who thought they could make a go of this rag?

One of us went on to become a very successful Artisan Carpenter and Design Consultant and now lives on a farm in a Kent village. He still writes in his limited spare time and had to be coaxed out of his workshop to co-author this book.

The other retired to continue writing historical books and trace his family history. Apparently only 500 people must die before he becomes King.

We hope you enjoyed this saunter through a rather unpleasant time in our lives and if you would like to know more, if we get enough submissions, we will start up a Blog to quench the thirst for this kind of knowledge.

The Commissioning Editors would like to aver that any resemblance to people living or dead to our Columnists is purely coincidental, I mean c'mon, nobody could be like them, and we hope to god they don't. We are so, so sorry for wasting your time. If we had known it was going to crash and burn this early we would never had started it.

But hey! We both got our £100 back as for the maiden aunt she can go and take a running jump!

The End...DEFINITELY!!!

Printed in Great Britain
by Amazon